# FREEMASONRY

# FREEMASONRY

## ITS MYSTERIES AND HISTORY REVEALED

GILES MORGAN

FALL RIVER PRESS

**Designed & produced by Alexian Limited**

Art director: Terry Jeavons

Designer: Andrew Milne

Editor: Fiona Biggs

Picture research: Vanessa Fletcher

Fall River Press
122 Fifth Avenue
New York, NY 10011

ISBN -13: 978 - 1 - 4351 - 0822 - 6

Printed and bound in Singapore

10  9  8  7  6  5  4  3  2  1

TEXT CREDITS

Scripture quotations taken from the **Holy Bible, New international Version**. Copyright © 1973, 1978, 1984
International Bible Society. Used by permission of Hodder & Stoughton Publishers, A member of the Hachette Livre UK
Group. All rights reserved. "NIV" is a registered trademark of International Bible Society. UK trademark number 1448790.
**Clement V** by Sophia Menache Copyright © 1998 Cambridge University Press

PICTURE CREDITS

**AKG-Images, London** 48, 64 Austrian Freemasons Museum, 101 Bibliothèque Nationale, Paris, 123 Bildarchiv
Monheim, 160L Ulstein Bild, 160R, 173, 181 Laurent Lecat/Musée National du Chateaux, Rueil-Malmaison

**Bodleian Museum** 98

**Bridgeman Art Library, London** 19 Lawrence Steigrand Fine Arts/New York, 30 and 145 Archives Charmet/Bibliothèque
des Arts Decoratifs, Paris, 33 Lauros/Giraudon/Musée Lapidaire d'Art, Arles, 42 British Museum, 46 Bonhams, London,
47 and 55 Torre Abbey, Torquay, 52 Archives Charmet/ Bibliothèque des Arts Decoratifs, Paris, 62 and 63 John Millar
Watt/Private Collection /Look and Learn, 88 Giraudon/Musée Calvet, Avignon, 89 British Library, 92 Christopher Wood
Gallery, 97 Private Collection, 99 Ashmolean Museum, University of Oxford, 107 Courtesy of Council of National
Army Museum, 108/109 and 110 Archives Charmet/Bibliothèque Nationale, Paris, 115 Private Collection, 121 Archives
Charmet/Musée de Grand Orient de France, Paris

**Cameron Collection** 13, 43, 57, 58, 104all, 152L

**Gettyimages, London** 15 and 17 Scott Barbour, 18L and 18R Grey Villet/Time Life, 20 Frank Fife/AFP, 21 Hulton
Archive, 22 Stefan Simonsen/AFP, 23 Stapleton Collection/Bridgeman Art Library, 35 Hulton Archive, 37 Bibliothèque
Nationale, Paris /Bridgeman Art Library, 38 Grey Villet/Time Life, 41 Archives Charmet/Musée de Grand Orient de
France, Paris, 61 Giraudon/Ecole Supérieure des Beaux Arts, Paris/Bridgeman Art Library, 82 David Silverman, 83 Julie
Cook/Photonica, 85 Chateau de Versailles/Bridgeman Art Library, 91 Christopher Furlong, 95 and 103 Giraudon/Musée
Crozatier Le Puy en Velay/Bridgeman Art Library, 102 Pinoteca de Brera, Milan/Bridgeman Art Library, 112 Hulton
Archive, 117 Bridgeman Art Library,  120 Musée de Carnavalet, Paris/Bridgeman Art Library, 125 and  138/9 Saul Loeb/
AFP, 135 Mansell/Time Life,  154  Stefan Simonsen/AFP, 155 Musée de Grand Orient de France, Paris/ Bridgeman Art
Library, 157 Ziegler/Hulton Archives, 161 and 162 Keystone/Hulton Archive, 164 Historische Museen der Stadt Vienna,
171 Pool/Anwar Hussein Collection, 176 Saul Loeb/AFP

**Jupiter Corporation Images**  45, 49, 50, 54, 67, 69, 73, 74, 75, 77R, 78, 81, 86, 87, 90, 118B, 119, 129, 146, 169,
170 both

**Library of Congress**  31, 126, 127, 128, 130, 131T, 132, 133, 134, 136/137, 140, 141, 142, 143, 147, 148, 149, 151,
152R, 153, 163, 166, 167 both, 168

**Private Collection**  6, 7, 9, 11, 12, 16, 25 and  32, 26/27, 28/29, 29, 34, 51, 53, 59, 60, 65, 66, 68, 70, 71, 72, 76, 77,
79, 84, 93, 100, 104, 105, 106 both,  109, 111, 113, 116, 118T, 122, 131B, 144, 152, 156, 158, 159

# Contents

# Foreword

Freemasonry is a topic that polarizes opinion. Much of the controversy surrounding the subject has centered on the perception that Freemasons represent a secret society with sinister aims and objectives that has wielded a powerful but unseen influence throughout history. Its many critics have labeled it as an organization that is, variously, corrupt, manipulative, self-serving, and even satanic. Those who have attempted to defend the reputation of Freemasonry have often pointed out that it can be more realistically regarded not so much as a secret society as a fraternal society that has its own secrets. Advocates of Freemasonry argue that the secrecy surrounding its rituals and meetings is mainly limited to codes of recognition within what its members call the "Craft."

Freemasonry is a global phenomenon and examples of Masonic-type groups can be found throughout the world. Many view Freemasonry as holding high moral aims and ideals. Membership is potentially open to anyone over the age of 21 with a belief in a supreme being. However, in order to become a Freemason, candidates must be nominated and vetted by existing Freemasons. For the critics of Freemasonry this process is indicative of the elitism and protectionism that is the true nature of the Order.

▲ The square and compass is one of the universal and most readily recognized symbols of Freemasonry and is often set into the walls of Masonic halls.

▶ A representation of the history of Freemasonry, which incorporates many key Masonic symbols, events, and people that have been associated with the Craft from ancient times.

Perhaps one of the most puzzling and perplexing aspects of Freemasonry is the way in which it defines itself. During initiation ceremonies candidates are commonly asked the ritual question, "What is Freemasonry?" The answer generally given is, "A peculiar system of morality, veiled in allegory and illustrated by symbols." Freemasonry also states that its three grand founding principles are "brotherly love, relief, and truth." Entrants to Masonic societies are very often required to progress through a series of ceremonies in which the mysteries of the Craft are revealed to them before they reach the rank of Master Mason. The circumstances and content of these rituals have led many, both within and outside Freemasonry, to question their origins and their meanings.

It is often claimed that Freemasonry is the oldest surviving secret society in the world, and the numerous beliefs about its beginnings seem to point toward ancient and esoteric origins. The origins of Freemasonry are obscure and uncertain but a body of different theories

has emerged in an attempt to answer the seemingly fundamental and basic question of how the Craft began. It has been variously argued that it derives from the practices of medieval stonemasons, that it dates to events surrounding the construction of the Temple of Solomon, and that it is connected to ancient mystery cults. One of the major and often disputed claims made for Freemasonry is that it is directly linked to the Knights Templar. *The Holy Blood and the Holy Grail* and, more recently, Dan Brown's *The Da Vinci Code* have linked Freemasonry to a supposed secret order known as the Priory of Sion, who are the guardians of the true nature of the Holy Grail. Freemasonry also features heavily in Brown's novels *Angels and Demons* and *The Solomon Key*.

The earliest written documentary evidence of Freemasonry dates mainly from the sixteenth century, although some have claimed that references to it can be found in older texts. The creation of the Grand Lodge of England in 1717 is often seen as a major turning point or event in the history of Freemasonry as the Order became more visible to a wider public for the first time. It has been argued that Freemasonry has played an important role in the shaping of American society and it is known that a number of key figures in American history, including George Washington and Benjamin Franklin, were Freemasons.

Some have claimed that Freemasonry also influenced the French Revolution and draw parallels between the slogan

"Liberty, Equality, Fraternity" and its own three grand founding principles. On a more sinister level, it has been claimed in recent years that the Victorian serial killer Jack the Ripper was a Freemason and the Brotherhood has also been linked to organized crime. However, it is perhaps not very well known that many thousands of Freemasons were persecuted and killed by the Nazis during the Second World War. Adolf Hitler attacked the Freemasons in *Mein Kampf* and regarded them as enemies of the Nazi party. Its members were barred from holding public office and arrested and interned in concentration camps as political prisoners.

In more recent times Masonic-type groups such as P2 in Italy have been involved in corruption scandals that have perpetuated the image of Freemasonry as a secretive and self-serving network involved in nefarious activities. Conversely, many Freemasons have pointed to their charitable work and their tradition of scholarly research and education as important and positive aspects of their organizations. Freemasonry can boast many famous and distinguished members throughout its history, ranging from Mozart and Sir Isaac Newton to Sir Winston Churchill and Buzz Aldrin. It has played an important and often little-known role in the shaping of western culture

◄ An illustration showing the dedication of the Temple of Solomon, taken from an old bible. King Solomon and the building of the first Temple in Jerusalem are central to Masonic teachings.

and, in this sense at least, its development can credibly be claimed to represent something of a secret history.

# 1 The Rituals & Symbols of Freemasonry

THE SYMBOLS OF FREEMASONRY HAVE PERMEATED OUR CULTURE IN THE SPIRITUAL, ETHICAL, AND INTELLECTUAL SPHERES, AS WELL AS IN OUR DAILY LIVES.

# Introduction

Attempting to answer the basic question of what Freemasonry actually is and the associated one of how it originated has proved a surprisingly complex and difficult task for both Masons and non-Masons alike. In 1984, following a flurry of interest in the Brotherhood, a leaflet was produced by Freemasons and issued by a group called the "Board of General Purposes." The leaflet, entitled *What Is Freemasonry?*, describes Freemasonry as: 'One of the world's oldest secular fraternal societies…a society of men concerned with spiritual values. Its members are taught its precepts by a series of ritual dramas, which follow ancient forms and use stonemasons' customs and tools as allegorical guides'. (*The Craft*, John Hamill, page 12)

The simplest definition of Freemasonry, then, is that it is a fraternal organization found in one form or another in a wide and varied range of countries around the world.

However, Freemasonry can also be regarded as a secret society in that many of the inner workings of the organization are not revealed to the general public. Freemasons aim to improve themselves by learning moral and spiritual lessons taught within the fraternity, not only to develop and benefit their own characters, but also in order to contribute in positive ways to the fraternity and to wider society. Its members traditionally share a moral code and value system with a belief in a single supreme being or deity. It is essential that prospective Masons have a belief in a supreme being or deity in order to pursue a course of spiritual growth. Provided that this criterion is met, the candidate is free to adhere to more or less any religion that they choose. One of the tenets of Freemasonry is that its members are at liberty to follow their own separate beliefs, but it safeguards this freedom by forbidding religious discussion within its meetings. Similarly, in order to promote unity and harmony among its members, discussion of political issues is prohibited within meetings. This has not always been the case, but, nonetheless, it is an ideal that is central to Freemasonry.

▶ Although Freemasonry is not exclusively Christian, as is often thought, belief in a single supreme deity is an essential tenet of the Craft, to which all aspiring candidates must adhere.

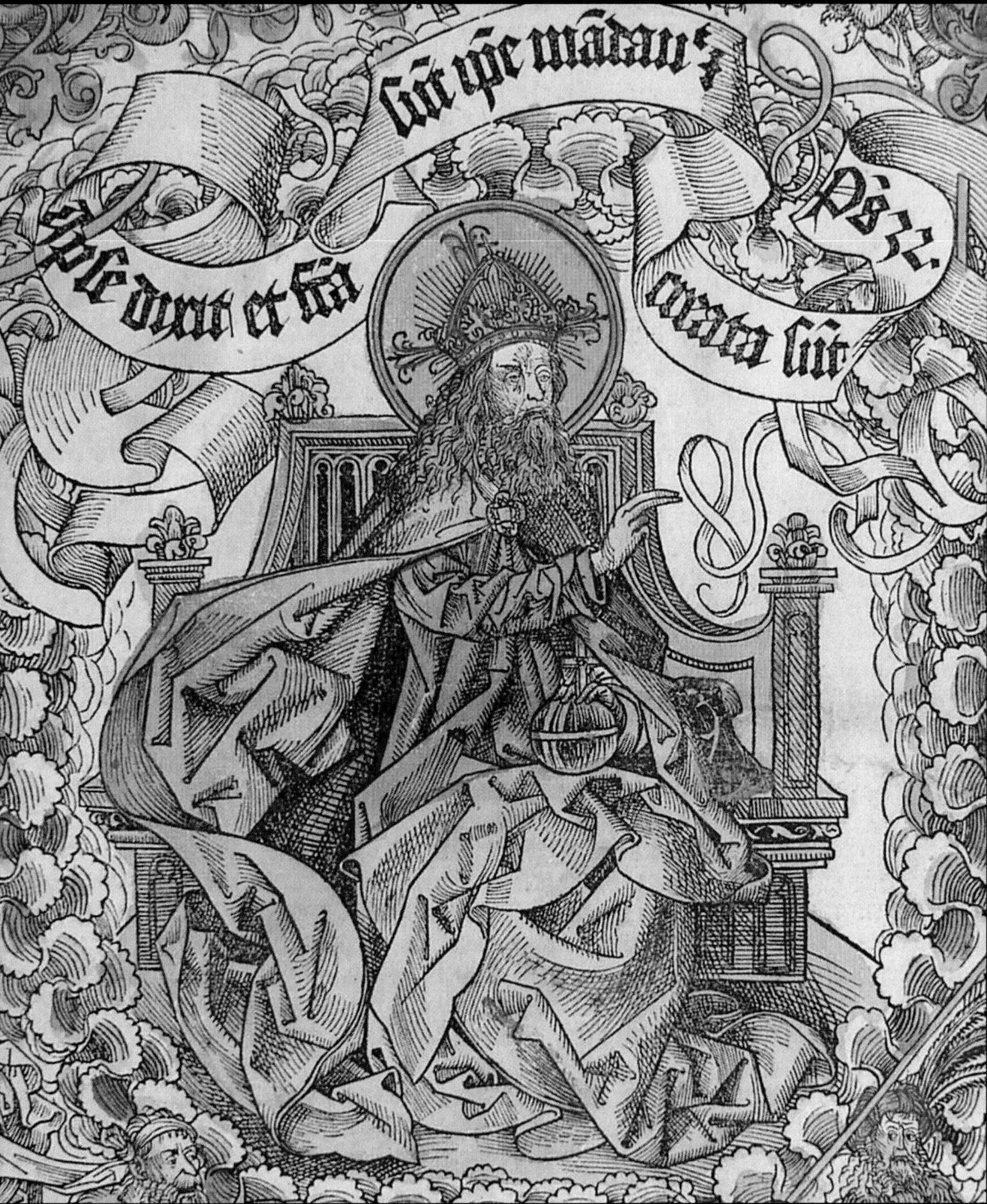

The vast majority of Freemasons belong to what is called "Craft" or "Blue Lodge" Freemasonry. Its members usually meet together under the guidance and leadership of a Worshipful Master and other Masonic officials at a local level. The officers of the lodge, led by the Worshipful Master, will initiate new members and deal with issues relevant to the lodge or local area. An important aspect of Freemasonry is that its members should contribute actively toward charitable and worthwhile causes.

There are three levels or ranks within Craft Masonry: the Entered Apprentice, referred to as the first degree; the Fellowcraft, which is known as the second degree; and the third degree, that of Master Mason.

▶ Freemasons Hall in London, headquarters of the United Grand Lodge of England.

◀ A graphic representation showing the three degrees of Freemasonry, as well as those of the later Scottish and York Rites on either side, all of which are attained by candidates passing through designated steps or degrees.

It is also important to recognize that Freemasonry cannot be regarded as one coherent and single body. Freemasonry today is the culmination of differing historical traditions and trends that will be discussed in greater detail in later chapters. Individual Masonic Lodges are governed by a Grand Lodge, which varies from territory to territory. In Britain there are different Grand Lodges for each country within the United Kingdom. English Masonry is presided over by the United Grand Lodge of England, while the Grand Lodge of Ireland and the Grand Lodge of Scotland preside over their members' activities. The central image or symbol around which Freemasonry is organized and teaches its spiritual and moral lessons to Masons is the building of the Temple of Solomon. Just as the Temple was intended to be perfect in its form and function in providing an earthly home for God, so Masons are taught that they must strive to perfect themselves and thus contribute to wider society.

# Masonic Principles

The basic principles on which Freemasonry is said to be based, and which are intended to inform the thoughts and actions of Masons, are brotherly love, relief, and truth. The principle of brotherly love emphasizes tolerance and mutual respect and working toward a harmonious and productive society. Relief is widely interpreted as offering assistance to those who require it through charitable donations and aid. The principle of truth requires that a Mason should strive to attain high moral standards and aim to fulfill his responsibilities as a Mason and as a citizen.

▼ Masonic principles were an influential factor during the French Revolution, with the revolutionary call for "Liberty, Equality, and Fraternity" resonating with the core tenets of Freemasonry.

Freemasonry instructs its members through a series of symbolic and allegorical moral lessons that are described as "degrees." It has been argued that these Masonic principles played a major part in determining the idealized qualities and beliefs upon which the Constitution of the United States of America is claimed to have been founded. It is also clear that the Masonic principles of brotherly love, relief, and truth had a considerable influence upon the ideals of the French Revolution, one which can be recognized in the famous Republican rallying call of "Liberty, Equality, Fraternity."

## Masonic Lodges

A Masonic lodge is the term used to describe a group of Masons and does not denote the meeting place in which they attend. The lodge rooms where Masons meet may vary in size or relative grandeur but they do share a core set of characteristics. It is important that the room in which the lodge meets should have an alignment running from east to west. Essentially, and significantly, the Worshipful Master is always seated in the eastern corner of the lodge room.

◄ The layout and symbolism of the grand interior of Freemasons Hall in London would be recognized the world over by Masons.

Lodge members are seated on benches along the south and north walls, which are themselves split into east and west groupings. One of the most distinctive and recognizable characteristics of the lodge room is usually the floor, upon which a black and white checkered pattern of squares features prominently, either as a rug, tiles, or mosaic. Conversely the ceiling often has a depiction of the sun or the heavens. On a practical level the lodge will generally have visible its warrant from its Grand Lodge, demonstrating its right to assemble and function as a Masonic lodge.

## Officers

The personnel at the core of a lodge hold seven positions; the Tyler, the Inner Guard, the Junior Deacon, the Senior Deacon, the Junior Warden, the Senior Warden, and the Worshipful Master. The Tyler's role is to stand outside the doors that lead into the lodge. He is

▼ A Tyler is shown standing guard at the inner door to the Temple, ceremonial sword in hand; and later seeking entry.

required to prevent any unlawful entry into the inner chamber and to make sure that the business of the lodge is not being over-heard by outsiders. The Tyler also greets all those entering the lodge and must ensure that Masons are properly dressed, usually in black suits with black ties and white shirts, before allowing them entry to the lodge room. Traditionally the Tyler stood guard with a ceremonial sword to stop eavesdropping or forced entry to the lodge. The Tyler's sword often has a wavy blade because, in the Book of Genesis, a flaming sword was placed in the east of the Garden of Eden to guard the Tree of Life.

▲ Adam and Eve are ejected from the Garden of Eden. The Tyler's sword often has a wavy blade, representative of the flaming sword in the angel's hand that can be seen in this painting.

The Inner Guard performs the same role as the Tyler but within the lodge room. Ceremonially, the Inner Guard will check that the Tyler is being assiduous in the performance of his duties by knocking on the door of the lodge, to which the Tyler must respond by knock-ing on the outside of the door.

Initiates are met within the lodge room by the Inner Guard, who escorts them to meet the Junior Deacon. The Junior Deacon helps candidates to prepare for ceremonies of initiation and monitors those who enter and leave the room during a lodge session. He must ensure that any who do leave or enter do so only with the permission of the Senior Deacon or Worshipful Master. He carries messages on behalf of the Senior Deacon.

▲ French lawyer Jean-Michel Quillardet, elected Grand Master of France's Grand Orient in 2005.

The Senior Deacon performs the same function for the Worshipful Master and has responsibility for the introduction of Masons from other lodges to members of his own. Within the lodge the Senior Deacon plays a significant part in initiation ceremonies, leading candidates and participating in ritual speeches. The Senior Deacon will generally progress within the hierarchy of the lodge and so must undergo training to prepare him for his next role in a "lodge of instruction." The role of the Junior Warden is to arrange the business of the lodge in terms of liaising with visitors from other lodges and, importantly, of covering the duties of the Senior Warden and Worshipful Master if they are absent. The Senior Warden is second in command and must be able both to help the Worshipful Master and to take his place in his absence and prepare for his own ascension to that role.

## The Worshipful Master

The Worshipful Master is the highest-ranking position within a lodge and must govern its business and ceremonies and play a central part in its rituals. He is the most important point of contact between the lodge and its respective Governing Grand Lodge. The Worshipful Master is responsible for the opening and closing of lodge sessions and for maintaining order and appropriate behavior within it.

There are several other non-ceremonial officers who operate within the framework of the lodge. Typically there would be around eight such officers, although, in some lodges, there are more. The least senior of these is the Junior Steward—his primary purpose is not to participate in the rituals and ceremonies of the lodge but to assist with lodge activities before sessions are opened and when they are

closed. The Junior Steward provides assistance to the Senior Steward and helps the Junior Warden with the provision of food and drink. Those serving as Junior Steward are seen as gaining experience and knowledge in order to progress within the framework of the lodge. The Senior Steward also plays an important role during meals, checking that everything is running smoothly, while also providing support and assistance to the lodge officers. All lodge meetings begin and end with prayer and it is the responsibility of the Chaplain to lead the lodge in this activity. He is also responsible for the safekeeping of the Volume of the Sacred Law. The Chaplain is, in addition, required to attend the funerals of Masons, where he would be expected to say

▲ Watched by a large crowd of onlookers in the Royal Albert Hall, London, England, in 1875, the Prince of Wales, a member of the British royal family, is installed as Grand Master of The United Grand Lodge of England.

Contact between the lodge and its members is the responsibility of the Almoner. It falls to the Almoner to alert lodge members to any of their number who may need assistance owing to ill health. Donations and links to external charities are maintained by the Charity Steward and he coordinates charitable fundraising within the lodge. The financial affairs of the lodge are the preserve of the Treasurer, who is expected to maintain exact and honest records of the income and outflow of the lodge's monies. The Worshipful Master will also

▶ A Freemason shows the set square and compass at the Logenhaus, a meeting place for women freemasons in Göttingen, Germany.

receive help and assistance from the Immediate Past Master who will be the predecessor of the current master. The administrative needs of the lodge are largely met by the Secretary, who deals with paper-work generated through meetings and links with other lodges. The Secretary is responsible for maintaining an accurate and up-to-date list of lodge members.

## Regularity

Freemasonry today is often viewed as a homogenous single global entity but, in reality, there are many different Masonic organizations, which have developed over time and through diverse circumstances. An important issue to arise from this is the question of regularity. Put simply, the Grand Lodge of a particular territory or jurisdiction must give its approval for a lodge to be considered "regular."

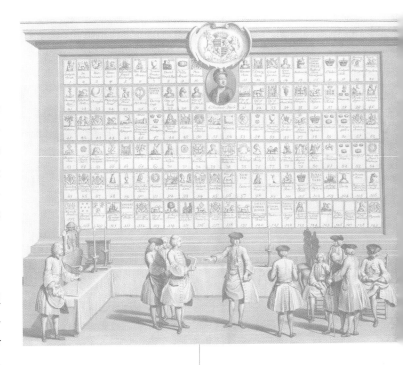

▲ An eighteenth-century engraving showing a wall of lodge signs of the 129 English Masonic lodges in 1717. By 1750, the number of lodges in England had increased to several hundred.

There is an obvious need for Freemasonry to monitor both its own activities and any potentially fraudulent organizations claiming an unjustifiable link with the fraternity. Together with the central principles on which Freemasonry is said to be founded, the questions of regularity and whether a lodge is recognized or not are widely regarded as fundamental to Freemasonry. Participating in irregular lodges would be punishable by expulsion from Freemasonry and so, of course, is perceived as an issue of considerable gravity. Different Grand Lodges are described as being "in amity" when they are in a state of mutual recognition, and members are permitted to interact officially at lodge level.

# 2 The First Degree

UPON THE RECOMMENDATION OF OTHER MASONS, AND
PROVIDING THAT THEY POSSESS THE NECESSARY QUALITIES
OF GOOD CHARACTER, A CANDIDATE MAY EMBARK UPON THE
FIRST OF THREE STAGES THAT WILL EVENTUALLY LEAD TO THAT
OF MASTER MASON.

# Introduction

In order to become a Mason, individuals must fulfill a number of basic requirements. They are usually recommended for membership by other Masons and must be of legal age. Depending on the jurisdiction, it may be 18 or 21 years of age. They must be without criminal convictions and be observed to be of good moral character. It is often stated that they should be "freeborn," an archaic survival that would originally have meant that they were not slaves. Importantly, they must also hold a belief in a single supreme being, with an associated belief in an afterlife. On this point Freemasonry claims to be non-specific and would be open to any monotheistic religion such as Christianity or Islam. The suitability of candidates is voted on by a secret ballot of the lodge to which they are attempting to gain entry. In order for a candidate to be successfully accepted all members of the lodge must agree on his suitability. Traditionally, during the vote, black and white balls, sometimes cubes, are used to register votes. A white ball signifies a "yes" vote and a black ball registers a "no." "Blackballing" someone, usually in connection with membership of an organization, is thought to derive from this Masonic process.

Freemasonry is most commonly divided into what is known as the "three degrees," or levels, of Mason. Many other higher levels within Freemasonry can be achieved, but for the vast rank and file of the Brotherhood, these three are the norm. The first degree or step in Freemasonry is that of the "Entered Apprentice," the second degree is known as "Fellowcraft,"

▲ An eighteenth-century depiction of the highly symbolic ritual, when the hoodwinked apprentice asks to be shown "the light" and is brought before the Worshipful Master.

and the third degree is that of "Master Mason." The first degree of the Entered Apprentice is marked by the "Rite of Destitution," in which initiates symbolically take their first step into the world of Freemasonry. Initiates are required to wear simple clothes, such as white cotton trousers and a shirt provided for the occasion, which are intended to focus their attention on their inner selves rather than on worldly status or wealth. They are typically blindfolded, or "hoodwinked," and all money and metal objects on their person are removed. One foot is fitted with a slipper, a state that is referred to as being "slipshod." Each initiate has his left leg bared to the knee and his left breast exposed. A rope or hangman's noose called a "cable tow" is fitted loosely around his neck and a sword or dagger is held to his left breast

# The Initiation Ceremony

After the guard has knocked on the door of the Temple, the candidate is led into the room. The initiate undertakes a vow of secrecy during the ceremony and he is led by the cable tow around the floor of the Temple. The reasons for the candidate being led around the Temple in this way are a mixture of practical and metaphorical concerns. Being led around the Temple in a system of ritual patterns gives the other members of the lodge the opportunity to see the candidate and ascertain that he is ready to undertake this next phase of his development within Freemasonry. It also has symbolic

▼ A candidate is raised after his symbolic death, his face covered, and swords pointed at his body.

value. The candidate can be imagined as threading his way through a labyrinth and being oriented within the world of Freemasonry. He is referred to as "a poor candidate in a state of darkness" and introduced to the Lodge.

During this symbolic ritual the hoodwinked apprentice asks to be shown "the light" and is brought before the Worshipful Master, who stands at the altar. When the blindfold is removed the candidate's attention is drawn to what are referred to as the "Great Lights" of Freemasonry, which have been laid upon the altar. These include the volume of sacred law, which is typically the Bible, but could be another text related to the candidate's faith system, the Square and the Compasses. The Bible is the guide by which Masons should live their lives, while the square symbolizes truth and the compasses represent knowledge and expertise.

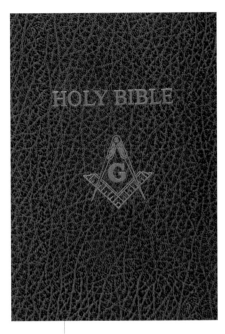

▲ The Bible is the guide by which Masons are required to live their lives, and an open copy is always displayed in the lodge when Masons gather together. The G in the center of the symbol on this bible represents Geometry.

It is interesting to note how many concepts and phrases that are commonly in use today derive from Freemasonry and its attendant imagery. For example, an individual who is believed to be reliable, honest, and trustworthy may be described as a "four-square fellow" or as being "on the level." Similarly, a commitment or deal might be described as being "fair and square." People commonly describe an individual who has been put through a rigorous or testing ordeal of some kind as having been subjected to or given "the third degree," a reflection of the gravity and seriousness with which the process of becoming a Master Mason is perceived.

▶ An example of a Mason's apron, which incorporates a number of key symbols, including the Pillars, the Square and the Compass, the Hexagram, and the All-Seeing Eye.

▼ A detail from a painting that shows a Mason working on the first Temple in Jerusalem, wearing an apron that is similar to the ritual apron of Freemasonry.

## Masonic Aprons

Candidates take a solemn oath of allegiance at the altar, laying out what their fellow Masons expect from them and what their responsibilities and status within the lodge are. Because the oath is sworn at the altar in the presence of the Bible or other sacred text, it is seen as a sacred promise sworn within the sight of God. At the next stage of the first degree ceremony the initiate will be presented with a white apron made from lambskin. This symbolizes the innocence of the entered apprentice. Different degrees within Freemasonry are represented by different apron designs. It is expected that the entered apprentice will fulfill his duties to the Brotherhood and society and conduct himself in a moral and upright manner.

Like the square and the compasses, the masonic apron is thought by some to derive from the time when groups of working stonemasons organized themselves into fraternal groups, and the apron, together with the square and the compasses, had a practical application. These stonemasons, who are credited with building the great cathedrals and abbeys of the Middle Ages, are referred to as "operative" Freemasons.

Over time Freemasonry developed into what is referred to as a "speculative" form, in that it became increasingly open to, and dominated by, individuals who did not actually work as masons. The role of the apron within modern Freemasonry is symbolic, and modern Masons see much of their work as inner activity and personal development rather than the physical labor

▶ An illustrated representation of Solomon's Temple in Jerusalem, which includes all of the key features that are incorporated into the design of Masonic halls in all jurisdictions and countries.

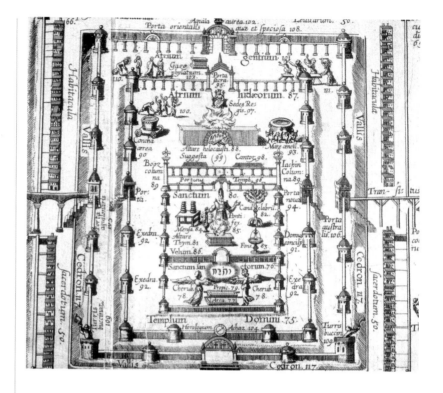

of the old stonemasons. The white lambskin apron also relates to the story of the building of the Temple of King Solomon and the unlawful killing of its chief architect, Hiram Abiff, which is central to the allegorical lessons that Freemasonry teaches to Masons.

## Working Tools

When the candidate has been presented with his apron the next phase of his initiation into the world of Freemasonry involves presenting him with the "working tools" of the Entered Apprentice. These are actual builders' tools of the kind that, it is said, medieval apprentice stonemasons would have used, but, in this instance, their value is symbolic rather than actual. The Entered Apprentice is shown a ruler known as a 24-inch gauge, and a stonemason's hammer called the common gavel. The symbolism of the 24-inch gauge, which is used to take measurements, is that it folds up into three sections.

▼ An example of decorative lettering, which incorporates a hammer or gavel and gauge, both traditional Masonic symbols.

The apprentice is informed that the gauge represents an individual day and that the way it divides into three sections illustrates the use that Masons should make of their time. Within one eight-hour section Masons should carry out their work or job, they should spend a further eight hours devoting themselves to their religion, improving themselves, and performing charitable works, and the remaining eight hours resting themselves through sleep. Candidates are then introduced to the symbolism of the hammer or common gavel and it is explained that they should work on themselves and their own characters. Just as the stonemason's hammer would be used to refine and shape stone, the apprentices must try to rid themselves of unwanted behavior or characteristics in order to refine and improve their moral worth as Masons.

## The Immovable Jewels

During the next phase of the ceremony the apprentice Mason is led to stand in the north-eastern corner of the lodge. The symbolism of placing the candidate in this area of the room is that it is traditional to lay the first stone of a building in the north-eastern corner and it is referred to as the cornerstone. Therefore the apprentice is symbolically creating the basis for the building of his own spiritual temple through Freemasonry.

▼ At the north-eastern corner of every lodge is the cornerstone, on which the stonemason's instruments are carved. It is here that the candidate Mason stands symbolically during the ceremony of the first degree.

▲ Identifying marks left by masons can be found on most of the great cathedrals of Europe, as seen here.

Significantly, the Worshipful Master sits in the east, because this is believed to be the place of light, the point from which the sun rises, while the north is a point of darkness for Masons. The candidate is moving toward the light of instruction and the attainment of wisdom, as represented by the presence of the Worshipful Master. The apprentice is shown the three pillars that support the lodge, which symbolize wisdom, strength, and beauty. In Masonic lore the three pillars also represent the three Grand Masters on whom Freemasonry is based: King Solomon, Hiram, King of Tyre, and the master builder, Hiram Abiff. The three pillars are shown to be linked to the roles of the three Lesser Lights of the lodge, the persons of the Worshipful Master, Senior Warden, and Junior Warden. The apprentice will also be shown the Immovable Jewels of the lodge: the square, the level, and the plumb line. The square symbolizes morality, the level represents equality, and the plumb line stands for goodness.

## The Movable Jewels

The apprentice will also be shown the so-called Movable Jewels: the rough ashlar, the perfect ashlar, and the trestleboard. An ashlar is a square-cut stone used in building and appears here both in rough-hewn form and in a perfected and prepared state. The trestleboard would, in building work, have been used to hold the plans of an architect. Within the symbolism of Freemasonry, the rough ashlar represents the spiritual state of the Entered Apprentice, the perfect ashlar corresponds to the Fellowcraft Mason, and the trestleboard refers to the work that a Master Mason should undertake in building a spiritual temple within himself. Tracing boards are another traditional tool used within Freemasonry for teaching and educating its members. They often consist of a colorful series of symbols and images that can appear surreal and bizarre to non-Masons but that have philosophical and instructional meaning for Masons. They take their name from the tracing boards used by medieval stonemasons to cut stone to specific shapes and dimensions.

▶ In Masonic lore, the three pillars are said to represent the three Grand masters on whom Freemasonry is based: King Solomon; Hiram, King of Tyre; and Hiram Abiff, the master builder.

# 3 The Second Degree

THE SECOND STAGE IN A CANDIDATE'S PROGRESS WILL LEAD TO THE POSITION OF FELLOWCRAFT FREEMASON, A LEVEL THAT IS REGARDED AS A SYMBOLIC COMING OF AGE.

*A Free Mason,*
*Form'd out of the Materials of his Lodge.*

# Introduction

The next stage in the development of a Mason is the ceremony of the second degree, where he becomes what is referred to as a "Fellowcraft Freemason." On a symbolic level the candidate is seen to be spiritually "coming of age" and entering the mature, adult phase of his Masonic development. Initially, the candidate enters the Temple wearing the white lambskin apron that symbolizes his status as Entered Apprentice. He is asked a series of ritual questions and provides answers to these.

Upon completion of this part of the ceremony the candidate must leave the Temple to don the same simple costume that was required for the ritual of the first degree and re-enters the Temple with his left leg bare and his shirt pulled back from his right breast.

## Symbolism of the Working Tools

Just as the ceremony of the Entered Apprentice features specific working tools of symbolic value, so the ritual induction to the level of Fellowcraft Mason is accompanied by an introduction

▶ The square is one of the working tools of the Fellowcraft Mason, and is symbolic of the need of a Mason to be upright and not to deviate.

◀ Present-day Freemasons wearing white lambskin aprons, which are similar to the aprons worn by working masons throughout history, and which, within the Craft, are regarded as symbolic of purity.

to more implements. The working tools shown to the Fellowcraft Mason are the three immovable jewels of the lodge, the square, the level, and the plumb line. The symbolism of the square within Freemasonry is that its two sides create a perfect right angle. In order to build a strong and stable wall a builder or mason must ensure that it stands completely upright, forming a 90-degree angle with the ground. The importance of this image and idea within Freemasonry is that a Mason must strive to ensure that his behavior and conduct are similarly upright and without deviation. Without maintaining this high standard the Mason risks a metaphorical fall. The level teaches Masons that, regardless of the circumstances of our birth, we are all equal within the sight of God and must work to improve ourselves both in the physical, material world and in terms of spiritual and inner development. The plumb line is a Masonic working tool that emphasizes the importance of fair play and treating others equally, and acts as a symbol of equal justice for all, untainted by unworthy bias.

# Symbolic Numbers

The numbers three and seven are significant within Freemasonry. Apart from the three degrees within Blue Lodge Masonry, there are the three basic tenets of brotherly love, relief, and truth upon which Freemasonry is founded; the three principal officers that exist within a lodge; and the three virtues of faith, hope, and charity, which lead to heaven.

The number seven appears frequently in Masonic ritual and in other phases throughout the degrees. The seven liberal arts and sciences are symbolized by seven steps on the winding staircase. The formulation of the seven liberal arts and sciences exists in many ancient religious systems where the number seven holds a special place of veneration. This is especially true in Jewish ritual and many Christian thinkers believed that to gain mastery of them was a means of achieving a greater understanding of God. They are generally said to be the subjects of rhetoric, grammar, geometry, music, mathematics, astronomy, and logic. The number seven appears frequently in Masonic ritual and in other phases throughout the degrees.

## Symbolism of the Two Pillars

Another image central to the second degree ceremony is that of the two pillars that appear at the entrance to all Masonic lodges and are a reference to the pillars that were set at the entrance to King Solomon's Temple. The initiate is informed that they represent strength and establishment and signify control and power within the lodge. It has also been argued that the image of the two pillars at the entrance to the Temple originated with the biblical account of the pillar of cloud and the pillar of fire that led the Israelites to the Promised Land. From the eighteenth century many lodges chose to place globes on top of the pillars, and, although there is no evidence available to

prove this point, some have claimed that such spheres surmounted the pillars of the Temple of Solomon. They are sometimes said to symbolize the two different spheres of earth and heaven. However, in some lodges, the globes were displayed on tripods close to the seat of the Worshipful Master.

▲ An apron worn by an eighteenth-century French Master Mason. The two columns Jachin and Boaz are featured with a group of Masonic emblems in the foreground and the Temple at the back.

## The Winding Staircase

The symbolism of the winding staircase is central to the second degree of Fellowcraft Masonry. This image is taken from the architectural design believed by Freemasons to have been followed for the Temple of Solomon. During the ritual of the first degree the ceremony symbolically takes place on the ground floor of the Temple. To advance to the next degree the apprentice Mason must symbolically ascend by the winding staircase to the middle chamber of the Temple. The image of stairs or ladders or even mountains within the symbolic language of Freemasonry is a common one, and denotes the ascent of Masons within the Brotherhood. To reach the second degree within Freemasonry means that the Mason is entitled to what is known as increased wages. These wages are symbolic and are represented in the form of corn, wine, and oil.

The symbolism of ascent within Freemasonry draws on the biblical story of Jacob's Ladder. During a dream Jacob saw a ladder that connected earth with heaven and God told him that the Jewish people would be given the land that stretched from the River Euphrates to the southwest. As a monument to the dream, Jacob took the stone upon which he had laid his head while asleep and set it upright. He dedicated the stone to God by pouring oil upon it.

## Symbolism of Masonic Wages

When the Fellowcraft reaches the middle chamber of the Temple he is due the wages of corn, wine, and oil, representing spiritual and mental wealth and plenty. Corn is, of course, symbolic of sustenance, since wheat is used to create bread, one of the basic foodstuffs upon which we all depend. Wheat also appears in Masonic imagery, woven into the shape of a cornucopia, often over-

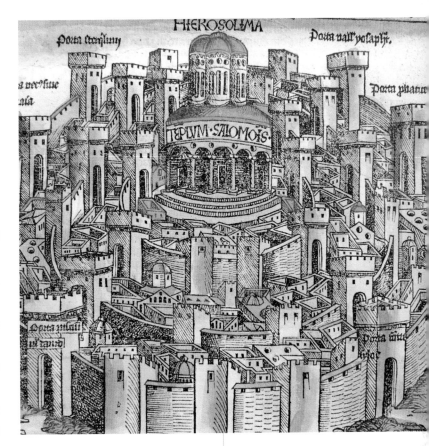

flowing with fruit and berries. The Senior Steward of a lodge, who has a non-ceremonial role, is responsible for refreshment in the form of food and drink during meetings and commonly wears an emblem or badge, described by Masons as "jewels," and featuring the motif of a cornucopia set between the points of the Masonic Compass. Wine denotes peace and good health and, in a Christian context, is arguably linked to the celebration of the Eucharist. Oil is believed to symbolize happiness and joy. For the Mason receiving these wages, they represent a just reward for leading a good life. The wages within Masonic lore derive from the "wages" or tithes that King Solomon paid the King of Tyre for the help he provided, in the form of builders and materials, for the construction of the Temple.

▲ The walled city of Jerusalem, with the Temple of Solomon at its center, in a fifteenth-century representation taken from the Nuremberg Chronicle.

◄ The symbol of the winding staircase is central to the second degree of Fellowcraft Freemasonry, although it is not unique to it.

# 4 The Third Degree

THROUGH THE FINAL DEGREE, THE FELLOWCRAFT FREEMASON
ATTAINS THE SUBLIME STATUS OF MASTER MASON. DURING THE
CEREMONY THE CANDIDATE UNDERGOES FIGURATIVE DEATH,
BURIAL, AND RESURRECTION.

nd en ainſi de quan / nre deuant dit. Quand ſalomo
uertus et de quants / ſon fil: ancores ieſune enfant eut
s il a eſte aucteur / prins le royaume de ſon pere. et fu
eulx de ſa ligneꝰ. et / aſſis ou ſiege royal. tout le peuple
q̃ quant y gt il eſt / ſolennelment fonent. comme en

# Introduction

During the ceremony of the third degree, when the Fellowcraft Mason is said to achieve the "sublime" status of becoming a Master Mason, the candidate is required to enact the role of the Grand Master of the building of the Temple of Solomon, Hiram Abiff. Through this drama the candidate undergoes a figurative death, burial, and resurrection. The Worshipful Master of the lodge narrates the story of Hiram Abiff, a legend that is central to Masonic ceremony, lore and culture. The theme of resurrection can be found in many cultures and legends and has

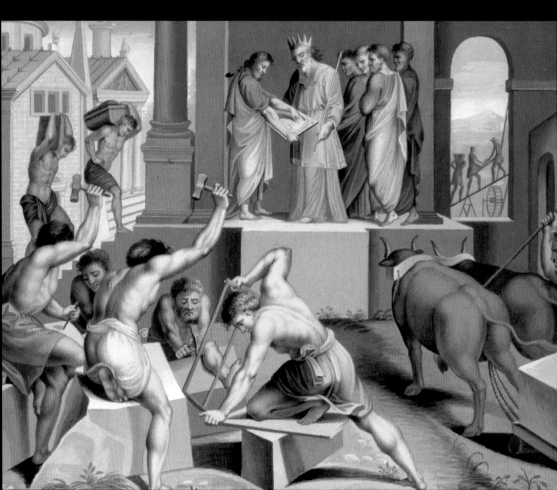

▶ An eighteenth-century painting for the Lodge of the Companions, which depicts the symbolic killing and resurrection that takes place during an initiation ceremony.

◀ An eighteenth-century painting depicting working masons building the Temple in Jerusalem, with King Solomon discussing the plans with Hiram Abiff, in the background.

fueled considerable speculation about the origins of Freemasonry. In the story that is related to the candidate by the Worshipful Master it is said that the Grand Master Hiram Abiff, who was the principal architect of the Temple of Solomon, was murdered shortly before its completion. As a Grand Master Hiram Abiff was in possession of the "genuine secrets of a Master Mason" and it is said that 15 Fellowcraft Masons junior to him formulated a conspiracy to extract those secrets from him unlawfully.

# Hiram Abiff's Murder

On the night before they planned to demand the secrets from Hiram Abiff, 12 of the 15 Fellowcraft abandoned their disreputable intentions, but the remaining three remained determined to confront their Grand Master. The three Fellowcraft stationed themselves at the east, south, and west gates of the Temple of Solomon while Hiram Abiff was inside praying to the "Most High" at the hour of "high 12." When Hiram attempted to leave the Temple through the south gate he was confronted by one of these lawless "ruffians," who demanded that he provide him with the secrets of a Master Mason and threatened to kill him if he did not supply the information. Hiram replied that only three individuals knew those secrets and that he could not impart them without the agreement of the other two.

The Grand Master offered words of encouragement to the Fellowcraft, suggesting that, in time and with his own personal development, he would be able to gain those secrets lawfully. However, he, Hiram, could not reveal them before that time because of the "sacred trust" that his position involved, even if it meant his own death. Greatly angered, the Fellowcraft struck a blow at Hiram's forehead that actually hit his right temple. The blow knocked Hiram down onto

▼ King Solomon discusses his vision for the Temple with his architect, with masons looking on.

his left knee. Staggering back to his feet, Hiram attempted to leave the Temple through the west gate but was met by the second ruffian, who made the same demand as the first. Once again Hiram refused to give up the secrets of a Master Mason and the man struck him a blow with a level on his left temple that, this time, drove him down onto his right knee. Injured and bleeding, the Grand Master finally attempted to leave through the east gate of the Temple where he was confronted by the third ruffian, who repeated the demands of his companions. Hiram remained resolute in his determination to fulfill his obligation not to reveal those secrets entrusted to him and refused to answer. The Fellowcraft then struck him viciously in the center of the forehead with a heavy stone maul, killing him instantly, and the body of the Grand Master lay sprawled on the floor of the Temple.

▲ King Solomon admires the newly built Temple, but without his architect Hiram Abiff, who has been murdered by three of his masons.

After the murder of Hiram Abiff, when the various workmen who had participated in the construction of the Temple met together, it was noticed that three of their number were missing. At this point the 12 Fellowcraft who had originally plotted against Hiram Abiff confessed the conspiracy to King Solomon and revealed all that had been planned. Greatly concerned by the absence of the Master Mason in light of what had been revealed, King Solomon ordered that 15 Fellowcraft begin a search for him to determine whether or not he had been slain by the remaining three conspirators.

▲ The burial place of Hiram Abiff was marked with a sprig of acacia, a tree that is associated with the themes of rebirth and new growth in Middle Eastern culture.

A date was agreed on which they should return to Jerusalem, and the men joined themselves into three Lodges and set out on their search from the three gates of the Temple. One group searched without any success at all and returned without answers. The second Lodge made an important discovery when one of their number, who was resting on the ground after searching for the Master Mason, dislodged a shrub from the ground and found that the earth in which it grew was loose and came away easily. Investigating further, they discovered the hastily buried body of Hiram Abiff. They then recovered the body, marking the place of its burial by sticking a sprig of acacia near where the head of the Grand Master had lain. In Middle Eastern cultures the acacia is associated with such themes as rebirth and new growth because it is an evergreen plant. Some traditions maintain that the crown of thorns that Jesus was forced to wear at the crucifixion was made from acacia.

Returning swiftly to Jerusalem, the men informed King Solomon of their unhappy find. King Solomon ordered that they should return to the site of the burial and create a sepulcher for Hiram Abiff that reflected his status and importance. He also informed the men that, because of the death of Hiram Abiff, the secrets of a Master Mason were now lost.

The third lodge of Fellowcraft had been searching westward and had happened upon the three disgraced murderers in Joppa. A member of the group heard one of the murderers, Jubela, wailing that he would rather have his throat cut and his tongue torn out by its root and buried in the sand a cable length from the shore where the tide passes twice in the course of a day than to be involved in the murder of Hiram Abiff. The second villain, Jubelo, cried that he would rather have his heart ripped from his chest and given to the vultures than to have played a part in the killing. The third villain, Jubelum, declared that he would rather that his body be cut into two parts and taken north and south and his bowels burnt to ashes and thrown to the four winds than that he be guilty of the murder of the Master Mason. The searching Fellowcraft who heard the lamenting killers took them prisoner and marched them back to Jerusalem where they confessed their guilt to King Solomon. As punishment for their crime they were all sentenced to the grisly deaths for which they had yearned. In Masonic lore the three murderers of Hiram Abiff are referred to as the Juwes, pronounced "Joo-ees." Hiram was said to have been reburied close to the Temple, and the 15 Fellowcraft who had searched for him attended the funeral wearing white gloves and aprons that served as tokens or symbols of their innocence. During the ceremony that echoes this story, the initiate is described as being raised to the sublime degree of a Master Mason. In the course of the ritual the candidate is actually physically raised from the floor by his fellow Masons.

▼ A nineteenth-century depiction of an initiate being raised to the sublime degree of Master Mason, echoing the story of the reburial of Hiram Abiff by the 15 Fellowcraft who had searched for him.

# The Master Mason

The working tools of the degree of the Master Mason are the skirret, pencil, and compass. A skirret is a pointed building tool that can be set in the ground and used to plan a true line from which to work. This, of course, is metaphorically extended to the behavior and deportment of Master Masons, who should use the religious teachings of their own faith system in tandem with the standards required of them by Freemasonry. The symbolism of the pencil lies in the fact that, while an architect or builder can use it in planning a structure, it also serves to record the actions of individuals.

The Master Mason must bear in mind that his actions will be judged by his fellow Masons and by God. The significance of the compass is that, as an instrument, it is used to determine calculations to a high

▶ A Master Mason's apron, rich in the symbolism of Freemasonry. Such aprons are often of high intrinsic value and are treasured items among Masons.

standard and thus it represents the role of the Supreme Being as the ultimate judge of humankind. The ceremony of becoming a Master Mason can be seen as representing the third phase of human life.

The Entered Apprentice relates symbolically to childhood and beginnings and the Fellowcraft symbolizes adulthood and "coming of age." The ritual of the Master Mason equates to old age and the gaining of experience and wisdom, together with a realization of our own mortality, accompanied by the comfort of belief in the immortality of the human soul.

The ceremony of the third degree of the Master Mason also includes a number of other images and motifs whose symbolic significance is explained to the initiate by the Worshipful Master. A pot of incense represents an individual whose heart is pure and a worthy sacrifice to offer to God. The Mason is told that, just as the incense pot glows and burns with internal heat, so should our hearts burn in gratitude

▲ In Freemasonry the bee is a symbol of industry, obedience, and rebirth; and the hive is a reminder to Masons that they should work to provide charity, relief, and help to those in need.

to God for our lives and for such blessings that have been bestowed upon us. The image of the beehive is a common one in Freemasonry and the Mason is instructed that it represents the theme of hard work and industry and the importance of dedication to our labors. Importantly, the motif of the beehive is also a reminder to Masons that they should work to provide charity, relief, and help to those in need, and emphasizes that this is particularly the case if it is within their power to do so.

The emblem of the Book of Constitutions, which is guarded by the Tyler's sword, symbolizes the importance of being perpetually aware of our actions and thoughts. Masons are taught to be cautious in discussing the private matters of Freemasonry and to be careful of what they say or reveal to others, particularly those who are hostile to Freemasonry. The symbol of the naked heart with a sword being pointed toward it represents divine justice that knows all and sees all of our actions and will reward or punish us on the basis of these. The symbol of the anchor and the ark draws on the story of Noah and symbolizes a life that is well grounded. By living virtuous and upright lives Masons will be protected by the safety and reward of a metaphorical ark where the soul will be rewarded after death.

The candidate is also taught to regard Pythagoras's theorem, referred to as the forty-seventh problem of Euclid. This reminds the Mason to understand and appreciate the importance of science and the arts. The Worshipful Master asks the candidate to regard the emblem of the hourglass and to recognize that, just as the sand runs quickly through it, so our lives are passing and

▼ Pythagoras is revered by Freemasons as a supreme individual who exerted a formative and important influence on scientific and philosophical thought, which Masons regard as two of the key seven virtues.

◄ An eighteenth-century painting for the Lodge of the Companions shows a figure holding a scythe, a motif that was designed to remind Masons how all human life rises and is cut down.

end. Our lives are short and so time must be valued and used well. Similarly, the motif of the scythe is a reminder of how all human life rises and is cut down. The Mason must understand and acknowledge that this is the final fate that we all share.

However, the brooding images of mortality and death are followed by the symbol of a sprig of acacia that reminds the Mason that, although our physical selves must die and be lost, our souls survive and live on. The image of the sprig of acacia comes from the Masonic story that it bloomed at the head of the grave of Hiram Abiff.

# 5 Historical Origins

ALL MASONIC RITUAL AND PROCEDURE IS BASED AROUND THE CRAFT'S ASSOCIATION WITH THE BUILDING OF THE TEMPLE IN JERUSALEM UNDER KING SOLOMON, WHOM ALL MASONS REGARD AS THE ARCHETYPAL LEADER OR GRAND MASTER.

שלמה המלך

The biblical figure of King Solomon has always been said to have possessed great wisdom and, for Freemasons, he represents an archetypal leader or Grand Master, who inspires reverence and offers an ideal role model. Solomon was the son of King David and Bathsheba. His mother assisted Solomon in becoming King after the death of his father in 961 B.C. However, it is the story of the building of the Jewish Temple named after him that holds the greatest relevance for Freemasons. The Temple built by King Solomon is central to the iconography and traditions of modern Freemasonry. It is described in the Bible as being the first temple to be built by the Jewish people in Jerusalem. King David originally proposed the building of the temple and, during his lifetime, he had made preparations for its creation. As well as gathering workers for the project he drew up plans for its structure. It was intended to house the legendary Ark of the Covenant. The Ark was made from acacia wood and gold and held the pair of stone tablets, inscribed with the Ten Commandments, that Moses had been given by God. It also contained the

▶ According to the Bible, the temple in Jerusalem was built on the very specific instructions of King David for the God of Israel. Solomon was chosen for the task as he had not been a warrior and so had not spilt blood.

◀ Moses is shown receiving the tablets of the Ten Commandments. Legend says that these were stored in The Ark of the Covenant, which was itself kept in the Holy of Holies in the inner Temple.

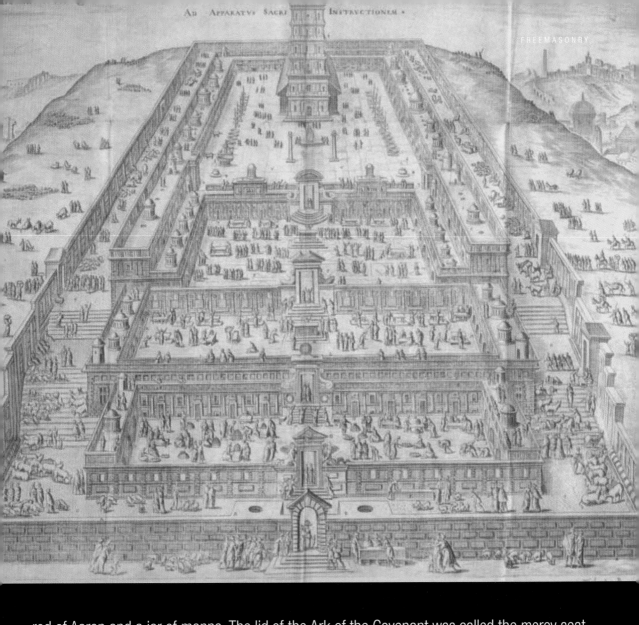

rod of Aaron and a jar of manna. The lid of the Ark of the Covenant was called the mercy seat. In I Chronicles 22 King David tells Solomon that he must build a Temple for the God of Israel and that he has provided him with one hundred thousand talents of gold, one million talents of silver, and so much iron and bronze that it cannot be weighed. He also outlines how he has provided stone and timber for the building as well as masons, stonecutters, and carpenters. In I Chronicles 28 King David gives Solomon not only instructions on the form that the Temple should take but detailed information about items that should be used within the building, such as

▶ At Solomon's request, great cedars from Lebanon were provided by King Hiram of Tyre, who had supplied them earlier for the building of a palace for King David.

lamp stands, bowls, and cups, and the weight that they should be, depending on the material used, such as gold and silver. King David reveals to his people that God had spoken to him and said that he could not build the Temple himself because he had been a warrior who had spilt blood. Instead God told him that he had chosen Solomon to build the Temple and that he would establish his kingdom forever if Solomon followed his commandments and kept the covenant that had been agreed with God. The Temple was to be built on Mount Moriah in Jerusalem, where Abraham had offered his own son Isaac as a willing sacrifice to God.

Solomon decided to build a temple for the name of the Lord, and a royal palace for himself. He conscripted seventy thousand laborers and eighty thousand stonecutters in the hill country, with three thousand six hundred to oversee them. Solomon sent word to King Hiram of Tyre:

Once you dealt with my father David and sent him cedar to build himself a house to live in. I am now about to build a house for the name of the Lord my God and dedicate it to him for offering fragrant incense before him, and for the regular offering of the rows of bread and for burnt-offerings morning and evening, on the Sabbaths and the new moons and the appointed festivals of the Lord our God, as ordained for ever for Israel. The house that I am to build will be great, for our God is greater than other Gods…. So now send me an artisan skilled to work in gold, silver, bronze, and iron, and in purple, crimson, and blue fabrics, trained also in engraving, to join the skilled workers who are with me in Judah and Jerusalem, whom my father David provided. (II CHRONICLES 2: 1)

▼ Once the Temple was finished, the Ark of the Covenant containing the tablets of the Ten Commandments was brought there to be kept inside.

# Hiram Abiff and Hiram, King of Tyre

The unlawful murder of Hiram Abiff, architect and builder of the Temple of Solomon, is a dramatic story that is central to Masonic ritual. The building of the Temple of Solomon, as recorded in the Bible, actually mentions two individuals named Hiram. The first is Hiram, King of Tyre, while the second is a certain Hiram-abi, who is described as a gifted master craftsman. It seems most likely that this is the Hiram described in Masonic lore. Hiram, King of Tyre, informs King Solomon that:

▼ Hiram, King of Tyre, who helped Solomon to build the first Temple in Jerusalem by supplying both labor and materials.

**I have dispatched Hiram-abi, a skilled artisan, endowed with understanding, the son of one of the Danite women, his father a Tyrian. He is trained to work in gold, silver, bronze, iron, stone, and wood, and in purple, blue, and crimson fabrics and fine linen, and to do all sorts of engraving and execute any design that may be assigned him, with your artisans, the artisans of my lord, your father David…We will cut whatever timber you need from Lebanon, and bring it to you as rafts by sea to Joppa; you will take it up to Jerusalem.**

(II Chronicles 2: 13)

In Freemasonry Hiram Abiff is often described as being "the widow's son," based on the following passage from the Bible.

**Now King Solomon invited and received Hiram from Tyre. He was the son of a widow of the tribe of Naphtali, whose father, a man of Tyre, had been an artisan in bronze; he was full of skill, intelligence, and knowledge in working bronze. He came to King Solomon and did all his work.**
(I Kings 7: 13–14)

▲ The building of the Temple would have required an extremely large force of workers, including masons, as depicted in this twentieth-century impression of the early stages of construction.

Work is said to have commenced on building the Temple in the fourth year of King Solomon's reign on the second day of the second month. This puts the date at around 957 B.C. The Bible itself does not provide very much more information about Hiram the master craftsman, and the story of his unlawful killing by the trio that comprised Jubela, Jubelo, and Jubelum as the Temple was nearing completion belongs only to Masonic ritual and to legend. King Solomon paid for the assistance of King Hiram with a form of tithe. In return for the manpower, the skilled artisans, the provision of the cedar and cypress wood and the other materials used in the building of the Temple, King Solomon provided food for the household of King Hiram. According to the Bible, he gave him a yearly supply of 20,000 cors of wheat and 20 cors of fine oil. During the building of the Temple, Hiram produced furniture and adornments made from precious metals, including an important pair of pillars that were set at the entrance to the Temple.

# Jachin and Boaz

The pillars cast by Hiram and set up at the vestibule of the Temple have special symbolic significance within the iconography of Freemasonry. Their important symbolism and meaning is explained to candidates during the rituals of the First and Second Degrees:

**He cast two pillars of bronze. Eighteen cubits was the height of one, and a cord of twelve cubits would encircle it; the second pillar was the same… . He set up the pillars at the vestibule of the temple; he set up the pillar on the south and called it Jachin; and he set up the pillar on the north and called it Boaz.**
(I Kings 7: 15-21)

Boaz, the pillar that stood on the left of the entrance to the vestibule of the Temple of Solomon and is recreated in modern Freemasonry lodges today, symbolizes strength. Jachin, the right-hand pillar, symbolizes wisdom and the act of establishment. When united they provide "stability." In Masonic images pillars are often surmounted by globes that represent the celestial and terrestrial spheres of existence.

As well as making the bronze pillars Jachin and Boaz, Hiram from Tyre, the son of the widow, created the "sea of bronze." This huge bowl-like receptacle was set on the backs of 12 bronze oxen with groups of three set at each corner of the compass. The giant bowl was around 4.5 meters in diameter and 2.4 meters in depth, and was able to hold around 45,000 liters of water. The purpose of the "sea of bronze," sometimes

◀ An early twentieth-century century Masonic tapestry containing graphic representations of the key Masonic symbols.

▼ An eighteenth-century copper engraving from Germany, which is an allegorical Rosicrucian design that incorporates Masonic symbolism, including the pillars Jachin and Boaz.

▲ An eighteenth-century engraving showing the symbols of Freemasonry, annotated to explain their ritual meaning and significance.

called the "brazen sea" or "molten sea," was to give the priests of the Temple a means of purifying themselves through the ritual immersion and cleansing of their bodies. Christopher Knight and Robert Lomas, in their book *The Hiram Key*, have argued that the mysterious figure of Hiram Abiff is in fact based on the real-life Theban pharaoh, Tao II the Brave.

As well as constructing the Temple itself, Solomon's builders made enormous efforts to provide the sacred site with the fresh water that was essential to the rituals of purification that were held there. To this end huge underground cisterns were carved out of the stone upon which stood the citadel known as the Haram, which defended the Temple itself. Water was conveyed to the cisterns by a specially constructed aqueduct, called the aqueduct of Etam because this was the origin of the flow of water. It has been estimated that one of the stone cisterns said to have been created by Solomon close to the Temple was capable of storing 12 million liters of water. Appropriately enough, this underground chamber is referred to as the "Great Sea." Work continued on the great Temple of Solomon for seven years. According to Masonic legend it was at this point that Hiram Abiff was killed. After resolving the circumstances of his death, Solomon continued with the construction of the Temple and appointed new trustworthy and loyal officers to carry out this work, known as "intendants" of the building, a title that can still be found at higher levels of Masonic teaching. The Temple was finally finished in 960 B.C., the eleventh year of the reign of King Solomon.

When the new Temple was complete, the Ark of the Covenant was brought from the tent temple called the Holy Tabernacle, where it had been kept, and was placed in the part of the building known as the Holy of Holies, the Kadosh Kadoshim. Before the Ark was put in place, King Solomon assembled all the people of Israel and they offered innumerable sacrifices of sheep and oxen to God. Once

▲ On completion of the Temple in 960 B.C., the Ark of the Covenant is taken from the Holy Tabernacle, to be placed in the Holy of Holies, the Kadosh Kadoshim.

▼ A nineteenth-century engraving, depicting the building of the second Temple in Jerusalem, which was begun in 515 B.C. on the site of the ruins of the first Temple.

the Ark was placed inside, a cloud appeared in the Temple and the building was filled with the glory of God. There followed a feast of dedication that lasted for seven days, during which prayers were said and sacrifices made marking a new chapter for the people of Israel and their relationship with God. The First Temple, as it is known, survived until 586 B.C., when it was destroyed by the Babylonians under King Nebuchadnezzar. The Babylonians took the Hebrews into a captivity that lasted until 538 B.C., when the Persian King Cyrus defeated the Babylonians.

The Hebrews, led by Zerubbabel, returned to Jerusalem, where plans were made for the erection of a new temple. A second temple was begun on the site of the ruins of the first in 515 B.C. When the Jewish leader Judah Maccabee took Jerusalem in 164 B.C., he ordered that work be carried out on the Temple as it had fallen into a state of disrepair. King Herod also carried out work on the Temple until it was finally finished in A.D. 64. However, this second temple was also destroyed in A.D. 70, this time by the Romans. Today the only part of the Temple of Solomon that still stands is the famous Wailing Wall, which remains a site of pilgrimage and veneration.

▼ The Wailing Wall, which remains a major pilgrimage site for Jewish people of all nations, and is the only part of the Temple of Solomon in Jerusalem that is still standing.

# The Search for the Roots of Freemasonry

## Hermes Trismegistus

Many of the written sources of ancient Egypt were said to have been produced by the ancient Egyptian demigod Hermes Trismigestus. Referred to as the Hermetica, these writings formed the magical education of Egyptian priests. Another text that has had a powerful impact on occult groups throughout history is the Emerald Tablet of Hermes Trismegistus. This work contains the philosophical idea that the pattern of the universe can be comprehended and understood through a realization that all things are interlinked. The text of the Emerald Tablet states that the wisdom of the whole universe is divided into three sections—astrology, alchemy, and theurgy, or supernatural magic. Hermetic thought, it is argued, need not be restricted to any one particular religion and need not necessarily be viewed as constituting a religion in itself, a claim that is also made of Freemasonry. It is, therefore, a philosophical system for spiritual development that can be combined with religions such as Islam, Judaism, or Christianity.

The Rosicrucian movement, originating in the seventeenth century and based on Christianity, was influenced by Hermetic thought and, it has been argued, had a significant impact on the development of Freemasonry. Within the structure of the Masonic Scottish Rite, the eighteenth degree is referred to as that of the Knight of the Rose Croix.

▼ Hermes Trismegistus, the ancient Egyptian demigod from whom the Hermetica are said to come.

## Pythagoras

A link has been claimed between the Greek mathematician and philosopher Pythagoras and the roots of Freemasonry. Pythagoras was born on the Greek island of Samos, close to what is now the coastline of Turkey, and in the sixth century B.C. founded his own secret religious and scientific society, the Pythagoreans, which may have been based on the cult of Orpheus. Pythagoreans believed in the transmigration of the human soul and practiced rituals of purification similar to those found among the Orphics. The Pythagoreans used the symbol of the pentagram as both a motif of health and knowledge and during initiation rites. The same pentagram device is also used within Freemasonry during initiation ceremonies and can also be found as a design among the so-called "jewels" or badges of office that Masters and Grand Masters of Masonry are entitled to wear.

▲ Pythagoras, from whom, some say, come many of the teachings of Freemasonry.

## The Gnostic Gospels

Christopher Knight and Robert Lomas, in their speculative study of the origins of Freemasonry, *The Hiram Key,* have argued that Gnostic thought may have played an important part in its development. The term "Gnostic" is usually applied to a body of early Christian writings that diverge from the teachings of the New Testament, as they are understood today. The discovery of preserved early Christian manuscripts, the Dead Sea Scrolls, along with the Gnostic Gospels, has caused considerable debate about the "true" nature of Christianity in recent years. In December 1945, a boy stumbled upon the Gnostic Gospels, contained within a sealed jar, buried in ground close to

▲ A papyrus scroll from Nag Hammadi, a town in Egypt where a large number of ancient parchments were found in 1945, and which comprise what is now known as the Hag Hammadi Library, or the Gnostic Gospels.

the Egyptian town of Nag Hammadi. The jar contained 52 papyrus scrolls written in Coptic, and are now thought to date from around A.D. 350–400. These texts offer a radically different interpretation of the death and Resurrection of Jesus Christ, in which the living are effectively spiritually dead until they undergo an awakening and are then viewed as having been resurrected. Knight and Lomas quote from the Gnostic Gospel of Philip, which makes this point, saying, "those who say they will die first and then rise are in error, they must receive the resurrection while they live." For Knight and Lomas, the concept of achieving a living resurrection can also be found within the Masonic ceremony of the third degree, showing that a link might exist between Gnostic thought and Freemasonry.

# The Essenes

A controversial and much disputed contention is that Freemasonry can trace its origins to the ancient Jewish sect known as the Essenes. This religious movement was in existence between the second century B.C. and the first century A.D. Most of what is known of the Essenes and their beliefs comes from the accounts of the contemporary Jewish historian Josephus. Josephus relates that there were three main Jewish sects, the Essenes, the Sadducees, and the Pharisees. Many have argued that members of the Essene community were the authors of the Dead Sea Scrolls. However, the term Essene is thought likely to apply to a number of Jewish groups who shared similar ideas and practices, but which also held divergent ideas on points of religious belief and practice.

It has been argued that there are numerous similarities between Masonic practices and what is known of those of the Essenes. Unlike the Sadducees and Pharisees, whose members were born into their communities, the Essene community, like modern Freemasonry, created its membership through individual invitations to join. Certainly it appears that the Essene community had different stages or levels of membership and that entry to these required candidates or novices to take vows of secrecy. Breaching these promises could carry terrible punishments. Masonic candidates who take vows to join the Order are also warned of horrible punishments that await them on breaking their promises, although these are understood to be symbolic.

▼ In a series of discoveries in 1947 close to the Dead Sea, a large number of scrolls was found in a total of 11 caves surrounding what used to be the site of a religious community known as the Essenes.

▶ Trajan's column was constructed during the first century B.C. when Rome's power was at its height, and when Mithraism was the official religion of Rome.

# Mithraism

Parallels have been observed between what is known of the ancient mystery religion of Mithraism and Freemasonry and, for some, these hint at a possible link between the two. The worship of the god Mithras in one form or another is thought to date back as far as 3,500 years, spanning cultures as far apart as those of India and Roman Britain. The cult of Mithras became particularly prevalent in the Western Roman Empire from about 67 B.C. until its fall several centuries later.

It has been argued that early Christianity and the cult of Mithras had a surprisingly large number of features in common, and that if Roman culture had not embraced Christianity, it could have become Mithrasian. Both religions feature gods born on 25 December who offer salvation through faith, knowledge, and compassion. Both involved a sacrament in which wine served to symbolize sacrificial blood and, during a ceremonial meal, small loaves of bread marked with a cross were eaten, symbolizing sacrificial flesh. Mithrasians referred to one another as "brothers" and were ministered to by a

▶ The god Mithras is shown fighting a bull. Mithras was originally a Vedic folk hero, and then a Persian God, and his cult was introduced to Rome in 68 B.C.

leader called "father." Although little is known about the theological structure and beliefs of Mithraism, it has been speculated, on the basis of written sources and surviving archaeological material, that its initiates passed through seven degrees or stages.

Mithraism and Freemasonry, then, feature the concept of its members passing through stages of development. They have also both served as secret societies in which special knowledge is limited to certain key individuals within the group. Both were groups aimed fundamentally at men. Many of those who joined the cult of Mithras were drawn from the upper echelons of Roman society, including the Emperors Commodus and Trajan. Freemasonry, certainly in Britain, has exhibited a similar tendency to recruit its members from the aristocracy and nobility. Mithraism was compatible with the old religions of Rome and Greece because it incorporated them into its worldview. Freemasonry does not claim to be a religion in itself and embraces a wide variety of faiths, seeing its purpose as the spiritual development of the individual within his own personal cultural beliefs. It can therefore be relevant to any number of different religions. Both Mithraism and Freemasonry have also stressed the importance of high moral standards in their members, although unlike Freemasonry, the cult of Mithras had an established class of priests who administered to the needs of its members.

## The Druids

The common claim that Freemasonry has ancient origins has, perhaps unsurprisingly, led some to conjecture that it may be linked to the Druids of the Celtic world. The Druids were the powerful priests of what are broadly termed Celtic cultures, which applied to large expanses of Western Europe during the Iron Age.

▼ Druids traveled far and wide, and were cultured and educated. They venerated a number of gods and goddesses and were known for their divinatory powers.

It is known that the Druids venerated a number of different gods and goddesses and saw many elements of the natural world as sacred. They were often called upon to divine the future and act as seers within their cultures, but it is likely that, Roman propaganda aside, they were learned and educated individuals with knowledge of science, the arts, astronomy, philosophy, and medicine.

Julius Caesar wrote that the belief that was central to their worldview was that, when an individual dies, the body may be lost but the human soul carries on and is effectively reincarnated in another body through metempsychosis. The secretive nature of Druidic rituals and customs, the memorizing of arcane laws, their powerful position within their respective societies, and their belief that physical death is followed by rebirth have all been linked with the world of Freemasonry. If a genuine link exists between the two it is unknown, but it is worth remembering that interest in the Druids was revived in the seventeenth and eighteenth centuries and it seems likely that ideas from the ancient past may have influenced the development of Freemasonry during this period.

▼ Druids were active across the
Roman empire during the time of
Julius Caesar, who had commented
on their belief that when a human
body dies, the soul nevertheless,
carries on.

▶ Stonemasons were a common sight in medieval Europe and thousands were employed in building the great Gothic cathedrals that sprung up across England, France, and Germany. Here, a medieval illustration uses contemporary figures to depict the building of the Tower of Babel.

## Medieval Stonemasons

Many have argued that Freemasonry developed from stonemasons of the medieval period, sometimes referred to as "freemasons." This may derive from the fact that these men were free to move from one work site to another, enjoying an independence of travel and employment, and were not the serfs of any particular lord. It may also derive from the French term "franc macon," meaning a man who worked in a lodge in the employment of the Church and was exempt from taxes levied on other tradesmen. Another explanation is that it identifies the type of stone that they were particularly skilled at working, being "free stone," a soft, chalk-based material. Those who worked in harder material were called "hard hewers" or "rough masons." The "free stone masons" were recognized as being more highly skilled craftsmen who were able to perform detailed and finely rendered work in the softer stone.

# Early Masonic Writings

The earliest known Masonic text to survive to the present day is known as the Halliwell Manuscript or the Regius Poem. It was "discovered" during the 1830s in the King's Library of the British Museum. It was subsequently published by James O. Halliwell in 1840. The manuscript poem is made up of 64 pages or 794 lines of poetic verse. Estimates as to its age have varied. A strong consensus of opinion puts its earliest possible date as around 1390 but some believe it was produced as late as 1445. Its Latin title is *Hic incipint constitutiones artis gemetrioe secundum Euclydum,* which translates as "Here begin the constitutions of geometry according to Euclid." Its opening section describes a legend that Masonry was founded in Egypt by the celebrated mathematician Euclid, and goes on to state that Freemasonry was introduced to Britain during the reign of King Athelstan. This English king reigned from A.D. 924–939. The poem relates how Prince Edwin was an early patron of the Craft and is said to have presided over an assembly of Masons. The document also lays out 15 articles and 15 points as to how the society should be governed, and provides guidelines for assemblies of Masons.

▼ Geometry is at the heart of all Masonic ritual and teaching. Here, in an early engraving, students in ancient Greece listen as Euclid explains its principles.

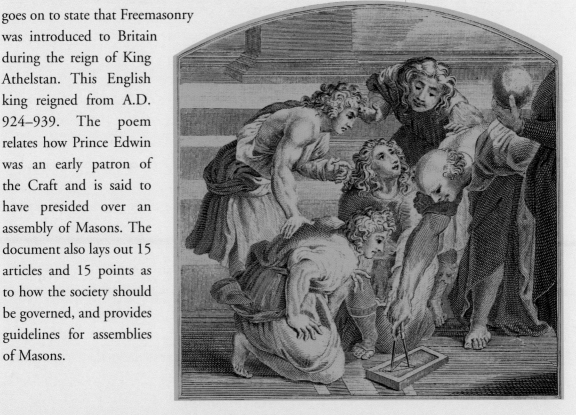

# 6 The Knights Templar

FIRST PROPOSED IN 1737, THE CONCEPT THAT THE CRAFT OF FREEMASONRY CAME FROM THE TEMPLE IN JERUSALEM THROUGH THE KNIGHTS TEMPLAR, HAS BECOME ESTABLISHED AS PART OF ITS FOLKLORE, THOUGH IT HAS NEVER BEEN OFFICIALLY ACKNOWLEDGED.

# Introduction

Perhaps the most popular and persistent theory about the origins of Freemasonry is that it has it roots in the Crusades of the Middle Ages and began with the military order of warrior monks known as the Knights Templar. This idea was put forward as early as 1737 in a lecture in Paris by Andrew Michael Ramsay. The Ramsay Oration, as many Masons termed it, proved to be very controversial and divided opinion as to its credibility. In more recent years many writers have attempted to link the Knights Templar with the foundation and development of Freemasonry, perhaps most notably Christopher Knight and Robert Lomas in *The Hiram Key*. They have argued that many parallels can be observed between modern Masonic practices and what is known about the legendary order of Crusaders. Supposed historical events surrounding the building of the Temple of Solomon are central to Masonic rituals. The knights took their name from that Temple because they were granted living quarters on the site

▼ The Al-Aqsa mosque, where the Knights Templar were given quarters, was situated on the Temple Mount in Jerusalem, on the site of the Temple of Solomon.

where it had been by King Baldwin II, the Patriarch of Jerusalem. Knight and Lomas argue that secret knowledge, passed down through history by a number of different groups, was discovered by the Templars on the site of the Temple.

▲ The ceremonial white gloves worn by Freemasons echo those worn by Templar clerics when they were consecrating the bread and wine of the Eucharist.

They also point to the practice of Templar clerics wearing white gloves while they were consecrating the bread and wine of the Eucharist and the fact that modern Freemasons also wear white gloves at lodge meetings. They also note that Templars would wear tight sheepskin breeches under their outer clothing as a symbol of their chastity and innocence. Parallels are also drawn between these items of clothing and the white lambskin aprons worn by Freemasons, which are said to symbolize innocence and friendship. It has also been observed that the battle flag of the Knights Templar, known as the Beausant, could be linked with Masonic symbolism in the modern era. This flag was divided into two vertical blocks, one black and the other white. For the Templars, the black section of their flag symbolized the profane world of sin, from which they had turned in order to commit themselves to the Templar Order, represented by the white section of the flag. In modern Masonic ritual candidates are said to move from a state of darkness toward the light of initiation into the Brotherhood. Modern lodge rooms also have a floor patterned with squares of black and white, and Masons are expected to attend meetings wearing black suits and ties with white shirts. If they fail to do so, they are deemed to be improperly attired and will be barred from attending lodge meetings.

# The Founding of the Order

The military Order of the Knights Templar was founded in about 1119 in the holy city of Jerusalem. Upon their inception they were known as the Order of Poor Knights of the Temple of Solomon. Their stated purpose was to protect pilgrims traveling on the road to Jerusalem following the Christian success of the First Crusade. Their founders were the French knights Hugues de Payen from Champagne and Godfrey de St. Omer from Picardy, who had both fought in the First Crusade.

When the Order was first formed, it consisted of just nine knights. These nine knights were given quarters in the al-Aqsa mosque on the southern edge of the Temple Mount where, by all accounts, the original group remained until 1127, when Hugues de Payen, their appointed leader, traveled to France to recruit new members and to

▶ King Baldwin II of Jerusalem assigns the captured Al-Aqsa Mosque to Hugh de Payen and Godfrey St. Omer to use as their headquarters. The Crusaders called the structure the Temple of Solomon and it was from this that the Order took its name.

◀ Bernard of Clairvaux, seen here preaching the Second Crusade, was a highly influential cleric, who gave the Templar Order its Rule. In a unique arrangement, he ensured that it was accountable only to the Pope in Rome. Several knights of the Order can be seen beneath the dais.

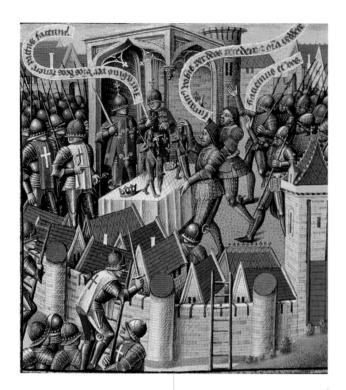

▲ Knights Templar fighting to retake Acre, which had been captured by Saladin during the Third Crusade.

have the Order officially recognized. Whether, in the intervening eight years, the knights had, as has been conjectured, discovered the fabled treasure under the Temple, or whether they had fallen upon some other object or information of immense value to the Church at that time, may never be known. But it is certainly on record that within two years the Order had—under the aegis of Bernard of Clairvaux, a leading member of the Cistercian order of monks— been placed in a unique position, being accountable directly to the pope.

But in addition to functioning both as a military force and a monastic order, the Order of the Knights Templar began, unusually, to grow to a position of immense wealth and influence throughout Europe and the Holy Land.

As their numbers rapidly swelled and as they gained donations of goods, land, and money to assist in their efforts in the Holy Land, or Outremer—"the land beyond the seas"—they eventually became the most significant military order of the Crusades. The Templars went on to serve not only in the Holy Land, fighting against the Saracens, but also in other religious conflicts between Christians and Muslims in Portugal and Spain.

In many ways, the Templars were like a present-day international corporation. They had properties and holdings throughout Europe, they were involved in manufacture and trade, and they also developed a an extremely innovative system of banking. Pilgrims traveling to the

Holy Land were able to leave possessions or money at one of the Temple preceptories or properties and gain letters of credit that could be reimbursed on arrival. At the same time the knights themselves appear to have led the austere life of monks, under a strict rule that had much in common with the Cistercians of the day.

## Charges of Heresy

It was inevitable that an organization of such wealth and influence would create enemies among those who were beholden to it, including the French king, Philip IV. In 1307, at Philip's instigation, the Grand Master of the Knights Templar, Jacques de Molay, traveled to France to meet with Pope Clement V to discuss the possible merging of the Templars and the other great military order of the day, the Knights Hospitaler. While this was being debated Jacques de Molay also requested that the pope look into allegations of gross impropriety made against several Templars, which had resulted in the expulsion of these members from the Order in 1305.

▼ A former Templar settlement at La Couvertoirade in France, founded in the 12th Century and typical of those which the Knights Templar held across much of western Europe.

▲ Jacques de Molay, being created Grand Master of the Knights Templar in 1295. By that time the Order was probably the most influential institution in Western Europe.

The incident had damaged the image of the Order and Clement wrote to Philip IV, informing him that he planned, reluctantly, to investigate the Templars. Philip had not been given any orders to proceed further but, on Friday, October 13th, 1307, he had all Templars in France arrested and charged with blasphemy, sodomy, and heresy. According to popular legend, the origin of the idea that Friday the Thirteenth is an unlucky day stems from the arrest of the Templars on this date. The motivation for Philip's actions is thought to have been a desire to take for himself the wealth and property that the Templars had accrued. Philip, who had a history of debt and insolvency, persecuted other groups within French society, including the Jews and the Lombards, and seized their wealth.

The French King had put considerable pressure on Clement, to condemn the Order but, initially at least, Clement was reluctant to do so and, in fact, had castigated Philip for his actions. He had quickly sent Philip an angry letter stating that:

**You, our dear son…have, in our absence, violated every rule and laid hands on the persons and properties of the Templars. You have also imprisoned them and, what pains us even more, you have not treated them with due leniency… . Your hasty act is seen by all, and rightly so, as an act of contempt toward ourselves and the Roman Church.**

(quoted in Piers Paul Read, *The Templars*, page 265).

The charges made against the Order had been met with consternation outside France but, faced by what appeared to be general admissions of guilt from the majority of Templars questioned, including Jacques de Molay, Clement had no option but to order the widespread arrest of its members and seizure of its property. In 1313, the final fate of the Grand Master Jacques de Molay and three other important figures within the Order was decided by the pope. They were declared to be heretics outside the cathedral of Notre Dame in Paris and sentenced to spend the rest of their lives in jail. At this moment Jacques de Molay, who was now about 70 and had suffered years of imprisonment, declared that the Templars were innocent of the charges made against them. He was supported by the Preceptor of Normandy, Geoffroi de Charney, who also recanted his confession. But Philip moved swiftly against the senior Templars in order to deny the Order any possibility of clearing its name. As relapsed heretics, Jacques de Molay and Geoffroi de Charney were ordered to be burnt to death at the stake. It is said that Jacques de Molay

▼ Jaques de Molay and Geoffroi de Charnay are subjected to a prolonged death by burning at the stake, on Friday 13th October 1314 recanting their admissions of guilt made under torture, and cursing the king and the pope to an early death.

once again protested the innocence of the Order and declared that Clement and the Philip the Fair would be summoned to appear before God before the year had ended.. Both the pope and the king died within 12 months. Interestingly, in 2007, the Vatican released a facsimile of the Church's investigations into the Order, which had reached the conclusion that the Order was entirely innocent of all charges. Clearly, King Philip's influence had ruled the day.

## Rosslyn Chapel

It is thought that the Templars may have had some forewarning of what Philip was planning against them. The fabled treasure that they were said to possess was never found, and it has been claimed that important relics and or documents were smuggled out of the Paris preceptory prior to the arrests of October 13th, 1307. One of the great unanswered questions about the Order is what happened to the fleet of ships belonging to the Templars, which was based at the French port of La Rochelle. It has been suggested that the Templar treasure, whatever it was, may have been taken to La Rochelle, from where an unrecorded number of ships left France. It is known that the fleet disappeared mysteriously but the final destination of the ships is unknown. It has been argued that a group of Templars fled persecution in France and headed north by sea to Scotland, where it is speculated that they found an ally in Robert the Bruce, who had himself been excommunicated by the pope, and that they went on to aid him in his victory at the Battle of Bannockburn. There is

▼ The French port of La Rochelle, from where a large fleet of Templar ships is said to have sailed, possibly carrying the fabled Templar treasure. Certainly no treasure was ever found by the king.

◄ The famous Apprentice Pillar in Rosslyn Chapel. In a story that echoes the murder of Hiram Abiff, the talented apprentice who made the pillar was killed by the jealous master mason.

a further suggestion that the Templars found a permanent sanctuary in Scotland and that it was their influence that resulted in the development of Scottish Freemasonry.

Many have argued that the architecture of the remarkable Rosslyn Chapel points to the influence and presence of the Knights Templar in Scotland. Rosslyn Chapel is located in the village of Roslin in Midlothian and was founded as the Collegiate Chapel of St. Matthew by William Sinclair. Sinclair was the First Earl of Caithness and a member of an important Scottish family, which was to develop strong connections with Scottish Freemasonry. The first Grand Master of the Grand Lodge of Scotland was also called William Sinclair and was a descendant of the man who founded Rosslyn Chapel in 1446. A number of other Sinclairs also held the post of Grand Master at later dates. The Sinclair family name is sometimes also spelt "St. Clair."

The design and decoration of the building has been the source of considerable speculation and conjecture and some authors find hidden meaning

▼ Rosslyn chapel is full of Masonic symbolism and it has been argued that it provides a tangible link between the Templar Order and modern Freemasonry.

and significance within the fabric of the building itself. The chapel contains many examples of carvings of the "Green Man." These strange carvings depict a human face surrounded by foliage and vegetation, usually with leaves issuing from its mouth. They are generally viewed as fertility figures and are widely accepted as pre-Christian. On the basis of archaeological digs carried out in the nineteenth century, some scholars have thought that Rosslyn Chapel was originally intended to be a much larger building. Some have put forward the hypothesis that the west wall of the chapel was actually intended to represent the Wailing Wall, the surviving part of the Temple of Solomon in Jerusalem.

Much interest has focused on three pillars within the chapel, which are known as the Master Pillar, the Journeyman Pillar, and the Apprentice Pillar. It has been argued that these, together with many other details within the fifteenth-century chapel, provide a clear link between the fourteenth-century Knights Templar and the modern Craft of Freemasonry.

# 7

# Freemasonry in Europe

RESONATING WITH EARLIER ESOTERIC TRADITIONS, FREEMASONRY
BECAME A MAJOR FORCE IN THE SEVENTEENTH CENTURY AND
IT HAS BEEN SUGGESTED THAT IT WAS INFLUENTIAL IN FRANCE
DURING THE REVOLUTION.

# Introduction

The development of Freemasonry appears to have had two main phases. The first phase was the establishment of the craft guilds of operative stonemasons who appear to have had comparatively simple rituals associated with their organizations. The second phase in the development of Freemasonry is the move toward speculative Masonry, where individuals from outside the profession of stonemasonry begin to be admitted to the lodges.

The Regius Poem or Halliwell Manuscript, dating from around 1390, is the oldest known Masonic document. The second oldest known document that relates to Masonry is the Cooke manuscript, dating from around 1450, and named after Matthew Cooke, who edited it for publication in 1861. The Cooke manuscript, unlike the Regius Poem, contains information of a speculative nature and is thought to have been written by a Mason. However, knowledge of the development and growth of Freemasonry from this period until the late sixteenth century and the seventeenth century is sparse. In 1425, it is recorded that a decree was issued on behalf of King Henry VI, who was only three at the time, forbidding English Masons from holding assemblies. It had apparently been noted that the working lodges had developed links that unified them.

The Schaw Statutes, dating from 1598 and 1599, give a fuller picture of Masonic practices in Scotland at this time. They are named after William Schaw, who was the Master of Works and Warden General for King James VI of Scotland, and detail the duties of lodge members. They ban lodge members from undertaking work with unqualified Masons, and reveal that Masons who produced work of a low standard could expect certain penalties. They also allude to Masons sharing knowledge of a spiritual nature.

Interestingly, the statutes also require that the lodges should test their members' abilities to memorize information. Information about lodges begins to grow around this time in Scotland because

► King James VI of Scotland who, unlike the English monarchy, allowed Freemasonry to function freely within the kingdom.

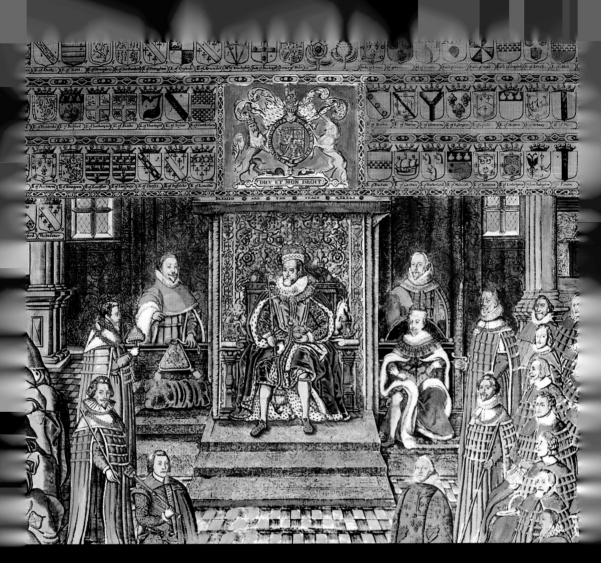

these statutes require them to keep written records. The Minutes of the Aitchison's Haven Lodge and St. Mary's Lodge, based in Edinburgh, have survived from 1599. It is recorded that Laird Boswell of Auchenleck was initiated into a Scottish Lodge in 1600. Because Lord Boswell was not an operative Mason, he is regarded as having been among the earliest known speculative Masons. In England very little documentary material has survived from before 1717. From this period onward Freemasonry underwent a growing process of gentrification

▶ Elias Ashmole's interests were extensive and included a fascination with the esoteric arts of alchemy and astrology.

# Elias Ashmole

One of the earliest written records of a Freemason being admitted to a lodge in England can be found in the diary of the noted antiquary, Elias Ashmole. On October 16th, 1646, Ashmole wrote, "I was made a Free Mason at Warrington, in Lancashire, with Henry Mainwaring, of Karincham, in Cheshire." Born on May 23rd, 1617, in Lichfield, Ashmole had a colorful life, combining an involvement in the politics of the day with a keen interest in alchemy and astrology. A royalist, Ashmole supported Charles I during the English Civil War. His major passion was acquiring unusual and varied artifacts. He later combined his own collections with that of botanist John Tradescant the Younger, and donated the material to Oxford University in 1677.

A building to house the collection at Oxford was specially commissioned and was designed by Sir Christopher Wren. The building was completed in 1682 and was named the Ashmolean Museum in honor of its donor. Ashmole appears to have maintained an active involvement with Freemasonry throughout his life, recording in his diary entry of March 10th, 1682, that he had attended a lodge meeting at Masons' Hall in London and enjoyed an impressive dinner at the Half-Moon Tavern in Cheapside with his fellow Masons the following day.

▲ Elias Ashmole, founder of the Ashmolean Museum in Oxford, was an influential and active Freemason.

# The Rosicrucians

It has been suggested that the esoteric Rosicrucian Order played an important part in the development of modern Masonry. The origins of the Rosicrucian movement have been debated almost as much as those of Freemasonry. Quite how the Rosicrucian movement began is something of a mystery in itself. In 1614, a Lutheran theologian named Johannes Valentin Andreae published an enigmatic pamphlet entitled *Fama Fraternitatis Rosae Crucis or The Fame of the Brotherhood of the Rosy Cross*. It describes how the Rosicrucian movement was founded by a German, Christian Rosenkreuz, who was born in 1378. According to the pamphlet, Rosenkreuz had traveled to the Holy Land and come into the possession of secret occult knowledge, taught to him by a number of Eastern masters. He is said to have founded the Rosicrucian Order in 1407, deliberately limiting its membership to eight. Rosenkreuz is said to have died in 1484 at the advanced age of 106. The Order was then supposed to have been kept a closely guarded secret, as its founder had wished, until it emerged on to the European stage with the publication of *Fama Fraternitatis Rosae Crucis*. Further pamphlets followed, the *Confessio Fraternitatis* in 1615 and *The Chymical Wedding of Christian Rosen Kreuz* in 1616. Some writers and scholars have regarded these documents as highly symbolic and allegorical in nature. The events they describe are not to be taken literally but need careful interpretation to reveal their true meaning.

▼ Lutheran theologian Johannes Valentine Andrea, who published the pamphlet *Fama Fraternitatis Rosae Crucis* in 1614.

◄ An eighteenth-
century German
woodcut depicting
the Rosicrucian Tree
of Awareness, which
illustrates the dualist
view of a world of good
and evil.

▲ One theory traces the foundation of the Rosicrucian movement to the city of Alexandria in A.D. 46. Here, in an early sixteenth-century painting, St. Mark is shown preaching there.

An interesting alternative legend describes the foundation of the Rosicrucian movement in A.D. 46 by one Ormus, a sage from the city of Alexandria. This version of the origins of the movement appears to have been put forward in the eighteenth century by a Rosicrucianist–Masonic group called the Golden and Rosy Cross. The legend claims that Mark, the disciple of Jesus, converted Ormus and some of his followers to Christianity. The Rosicrucian Order, therefore, was based on a fusion of early Christian teaching and Egyptian beliefs and ideas. The story of Christian Rosenkreuz is incorporated into this series of events when he becomes the Grand Master of the existing Rosicrucian Order. It has been conjectured by some that the secret knowledge that Christian Rosenkreuz was said to have gained in the first theory of the origins of Rosicrucianism could have been absorbed into Freemasonry. While traveling in the Holy Land he could have learned from the Eastern masters the stories and legends of the Temple of Solomon, and, upon his return to Europe, shared that knowledge within the secret order. That knowledge could, in turn, have been transmitted to the developing Masonic Order via an initiate and become part of its rituals and iconography. Although such speculative thought has fired the interest of many, it seems that the "emergence" of the Rosicrucian movement may, in fact, have an altogether more mundane explanation. The author of the pamphlets, Johannes Valentin Andreae, would later explain that he had intended the documents to be viewed as a kind of farce or drama designed to make an allegorical point.

Andreae was a Lutheran theologian and, as a Protestant, he believed that a society freed from the restrictions and restraints of the Roman Catholic Church would be able to explore more freely such subjects as alchemy and science, thus aiding humankind in the pursuit of a new, more Utopian era. However, whatever the rationale behind the pamphlets may have been, the ideas contained within them provoked much interest in seventeenth-century Europe, although there is no evidence that an actual secret society existed before the publication of the papers. Freemasons were certainly interested in the ideas inherent within Rosicrucianism and, in some instances, incorporated the image of the rose and cross in their iconography. It has been suggested that there are similarities between the aims of Freemasonry and its attempts to effect a kind of spiritual, alchemical change in the worldview of individual Masons, and the mystical goals of the Rosicrucian movement in developing human potential through mystical study. In the Masonic Scottish Rite the Knight of the Rose Croix degree is the eighteenth degree or stage of development. In addition, there exists a Masonic group, the Order of Masonic Rosicrucians, which is open to Master Masons through invitation. The Order focuses particularly on the Rosicrucian documents and studies them along with other mystical teachings, such as the Hermetic tradition.

▼ A nineteenth-century French apron of a master of the Rose-Croix, the second chapter of the Scottish Rite of Freemasonry.

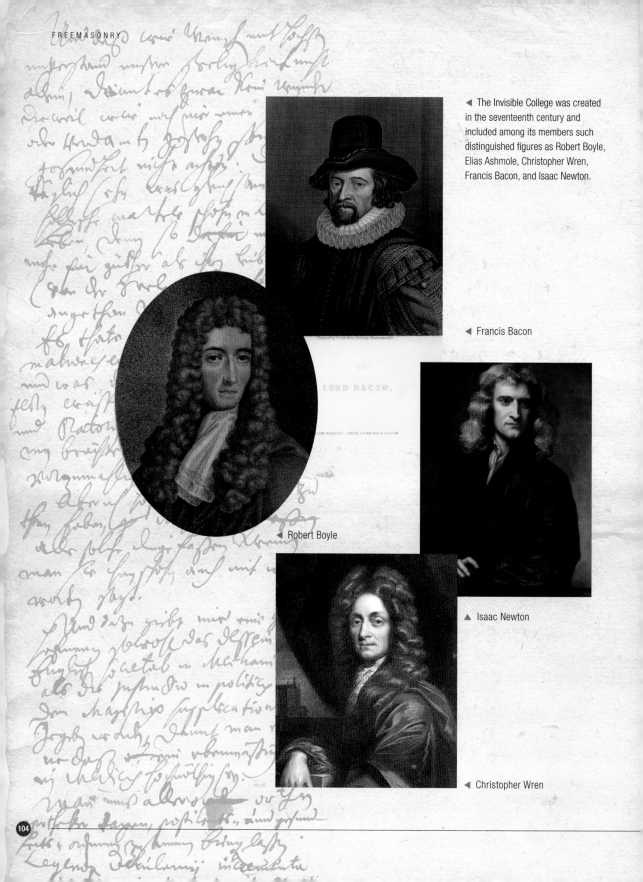

◀ The Invisible College was created in the seventeenth century and included among its members such distinguished figures as Robert Boyle, Elias Ashmole, Christopher Wren, Francis Bacon, and Isaac Newton.

◀ Francis Bacon

◀ Robert Boyle

▲ Isaac Newton

◀ Christopher Wren

## The Invisible College

One of the most influential groups during the Renaissance period that involved active Freemasons was the so-called Invisible College. This society of scientists and philosophers was created in the seventeenth century and included amongst its members such distinguished figures as Robert Boyle, Elias Ashmole, Christopher Wren, Francis Bacon, and Isaac Newton. The society offered a forum for discussion and the mutual exchange of ideas on subjects that would have included science, alchemy, and assorted esoteric ideas. However, the religious and political climate of the time meant that the discussion of such issues was potentially a dangerous undertaking. Scientists such as Galileo had provoked the ire of the Roman Catholic Church by suggesting that the earth moved around the sun, and those found guilty of heresy could be burned to death at the stake. In England the turmoil of the Civil War and the paranoia of Puritanism led to the appalling witch hunts with which that period is associated.

▼ The present-day Royal Society building in central London.

It was vital therefore that the exchange of such information be concealed within the framework of the Invisible College. It has been suggested that the move from operative to speculative Freemasonry may have taken place during this period because the secrecy of the operative stonemasons' guilds provided secure meeting places for freethinkers and philosophers. By veiling their intellectual pursuits in allegory, it was possible to avoid the suspicions of state and Church. The Invisible College emerged into the open when, in 1662, Charles II granted them the privilege of a royal charter. It would form the basis for the subsequent creation of the Royal Society.

# Freemasonry after 1717

▼ The Goose and Gridiron tavern in London where, in 1717, the combined lodge that would become the Grand Lodge of England, first met.

The Goose and Gridiron tavern in London where, in 1717, the combined lodge that would become the Grand Lodge of England, first met.

The year 1717 is a key date in the history of Freemasonry and was when the Craft became much more publicly visible and recognized organization. Four London lodges took the decision to form one "Grand Lodge," which would subsequently act as the presiding head of all English Lodges. The four lodges had previously met in taverns and alehouses around the city. The Goose and Gridiron Alehouse, close to St. Paul's Cathedral, had been the meeting point for Lodge No.1, while Lodge No.2 had convened at the Crown, close to Drury Lane. The members of Lodge No.3 held their meetings at the Apple Tree Tavern in Covent Garden, and Lodge No. 4 met at a tavern in Westminster called the Rummer and Grapes. The separate lodges met in the Apple Tree Tavern in February 1717, where it was agreed that they would be combined to become the Grand Lodge of England, or GLE. On the feast of St. John the Baptist, June 24th, 1717, the combined lodge met at the Goose and Gridiron and elected their first Grand Master, Anthony Sayer. The Grand Lodge appeared to go from strength to strength and, in 1721, altered its title to the Premier Grand Lodge of England. By that time, it was head of over 50 lodges in and around London.

John Duke of Montague K.G.
Mas.r Gen.l of the Ordinance.
Ob.1749.

They elected the Duke of Montague as their Grand Master, which was something of a departure for a movement that had not, as a rule, previously elected individuals from the aristocracy. Dr. James Anderson, a Freemason of Scottish descent, produced and had published the Constitutions of the Freemasons in 1723. The full title of this important Masonic document is "The Constitution, History, Laws, Charges, Orders, Regulations, and Usages, of the Right

Engrav'd by John Pine in Aldersgate Street London

Worshipful Fraternity of Accepted Free Masons; collected from their general Records, and their faithful traditions of many Ages."

One of James Anderson's greatest innovations in his interpretation of the rules and history of Freemasonry was his shift of the religious emphasis of the Brotherhood away from a specifically Christian doctrine. He paved the way for modern Freemasonry's more generalized concept of a universal God with the insertion of the statement that Masons should recognize "that religion in which all men agree," and

# THE
# CONSTITUTIONS
### OF THE
# FREE-MASONS.

### CONTAINING THE

*History, Charges, Regulations, &c.*
of that moft Ancient and Right
Worfhipful *FRATERNITY.*

For the Ufe of the LODGES.

*LONDON:*

Printed by WILLIAM HUNTER, for JOHN SENEX at the *Globe,*
and JOHN HOOKE at the *Flower-de-luce* over-againft *St. Dunftan's*
*Church,* in *Fleet-ftreet.*

In the Year of Mafonry ———— 5723;
*Anno Domini* ———— 1723,

◄ The constitutions of the Freemasons, by Dr. James Anderson,
published in London in 1723.
The engraving shows John, Duke
of Montague, Grand Master of
the Freemasons, presenting the
compass and the roll of constitutions
to Philip, Duke of Wharton.

▼ James Anderson had suggested
that the secrets of Freemasonry
were passed to Moses from Noah,
and thence onward, a theory that
has generally been accepted as
imaginative invention.

by establishing in written form the concept of a "Great Architect of
the Universe," drawing on the inherent iconography of Freemasonry
itself and the symbolism of building and design. However, Anderson's
history, which argues that the secrets of Freemasonry had passed
from Noah and that Moses had been a Mason, has generally been
accepted as imaginative invention. Anderson also concluded that
Hiram Abiff had been an actual historical figure, and was chief
architect at the building of the Temple of King Solomon, exactly as

There has been considerable speculation about the reasons for the creation of the Grand Lodge, and its subsequent growth and influence and associations with powerful and aristocratic members of society. In *The Temple and the Lodge*, Michael Baigent and Richard Leigh argue that it was a consequence of the failed Jacobite revolution of 1715 and the House of Hanover's retention of power in England. Because Freemasonry had strong links with Scotland and, in the authors' opinion, was inseparable from the Stuart cause, there was a fear that it could be seen as a threat to the English monarchy. In France, where many Jacobites had sought shelter in previous years, evidence suggests that Freemasonry was in favor of the restoration of the Stuarts in England. By forming the Grand Lodge, English Masons were attempting to take an impartial stance. They were stressing that they were neither politically nor religiously partisan and were aligning themselves with the establishment of the day. By placing high-ranking members of the aristocracy in its most senior positions, Freemasonry was effectively declaring that it posed no disruptive threat to society. In the next few decades Ireland and Scotland would follow suit, forming their own Grand Lodges.

During this period, Freemasonry continued to develop into the form in which it is now recognized. A notable example of this development is the introduction of the third degree of Master Mason in around 1725. The ritual of the third degree is thought

▼ Freemasons learn of the establishment of a Chapter of the Rose Cross in Arras, France, by Charles Edward Stuart, pretender to the English crown.

by some to have been instigated by a former Grand Master, John Theophilus Desaguliers. The third degree of the Master Mason was officially accepted by the Grand Lodge in 1738 when Anderson's revised Constitutions were accepted. Although the Grand Lodge of England had grown in status, there remained large groups of Masons that operated outside the influence of the newly created body. These "Old Masons" tended to be from working-class backgrounds and felt a sense of separation from the increasingly aristocratic nature of the Grand Lodge of England. Many Irish and Scottish Masons felt that they had little in common with the reconstituted GLE, which had, they believed, moved away from what they considered to be an "ancient" and more authentic form of Freemasonry.

▲ Grand Master John Theophilus Desguilers, who instigated the third degree of Master Mason in 1725.

The working-class Masons of London forged greater links with Scottish and Irish Masons in London until, on July 17th, 1751, a rival Grand Lodge was constituted. Members of five different lodges assembled in the Turk's Head Tavern, at that time located on Greek Street in Soho, and took the step of forming an alternative body to the GLE, which they called "The Most Ancient and Honourable Society of Free and Accepted Masons." Because of their belief that they represented an older, more undiluted form of Freemasonry, they referred to themselves as "the Ancients," and dubbed the Grand Lodge of England "the Moderns."

The formation of the rival Grand Lodge appeared to create a schism within English Masonry for over half a century, although later Masonic historians were quick to point out that the majority of those belonging to the Ancients were, in fact, Irish rather than English. However, in 1813, the two factions were finally reconciled, and the two groups were merged to create the United Grand Lodge of England. The new body thus formed from the rival groups tended to favor the Ancients' approach to Masonic ceremonies and rituals.

# The French Revolution

Michael Baigent and Richard Leigh have suggested that Freemasonry first arrived in France between 1688 and 1691 with what remained of the Jacobite army of James II. However, the first reliable and unequivocal documentation for the founding of a French Masonic lodge dates from 1725. It is known that in 1728, a number of French lodges formed the English Grand Lodge of France. The first Grand Master of the newly created body was the Duke of Wharton, who had previously served as the Grand Master of the Grand Lodge of England. In 1737, Andrew Michael Ramsay delivered the famous "Ramsay Oration" in Paris. His argument that Freemasonry had its origins in the Holy Land at the time of the Crusades and that it had survived in Scotland right through to the eighteenth century was very popular and influential in France.

▼ King James II escapes to France with the remnants of his Jacobite army, which group, it has been suggested, introduced Freemasonry to France.

The Arms of ẏ most Ancient & Honorable Fraternity of Free and Accepted Masons

Holiness to the Lord.

The Arms of the Operative, or Stone Masons

Larken Sculp.

L. HYNEMAN.

MASONIC LIBRARY.

T. Sinclair's lith. Phila.

▶ The frontispiece from *Ahiman Rezon*, published in England in 1764 by a group dubbed the "moderns" suggests that they were in fact less speculative Freemasons, and more stonecutters. Similar splits would appear soon afterward in France.

However, in 1737, King Louis XV of France banned Freemasonry amid paranoid anxiety that it might serve as a source of secret plotting among the aristocracy against him. The Catholic Church was also, and remains today, strongly opposed to Freemasonry, and, while it flourished in Protestant England, it was attacked by the Vatican. The first Papal condemnation of Freemasonry was issued on April 28th, 1738, by Pope Clement XII. In his papal bull the pope stated that:

**Now it has come to Our ears, and common gossip has made clear, that certain Societies, Companies, Assemblies, Meetings, Congregations or Conventicles called in the popular tongue Liberi Muratori or Francs Massons or by other names according to the various languages, are spreading far and wide and daily growing in strength: and men of any Religion or sect, satisfied with the appearance of natural probity, are joined together, according to the laws and the statutes laid down for them, by a strict and unbreakable bond which obligates them, both by an oath upon the Holy Bible and by a host of grievous punishments, to an inviolable silence about all that they do in secret together. But it is in the nature of the crime to betray itself and show itself by its attendant clamor. Thus these aforesaid Societies or Conventicles have caused in the minds of the faithful the greatest suspicion, and all prudent and upright men have passed the same judgment on them as being depraved and perverted.**

Despite the ban of 1737, and the fact that Pope Clement XII also condemned Freemasonry and threatened excommunication to any who joined it in his papal bull of 1738, the Craft continued to thrive and grow in France. Many Masonic lodges in France followed the Ancient Scottish Rite popularized by Ramsay. In 1756, French Masonry was divided when the English Grand Lodge of France declared itself to

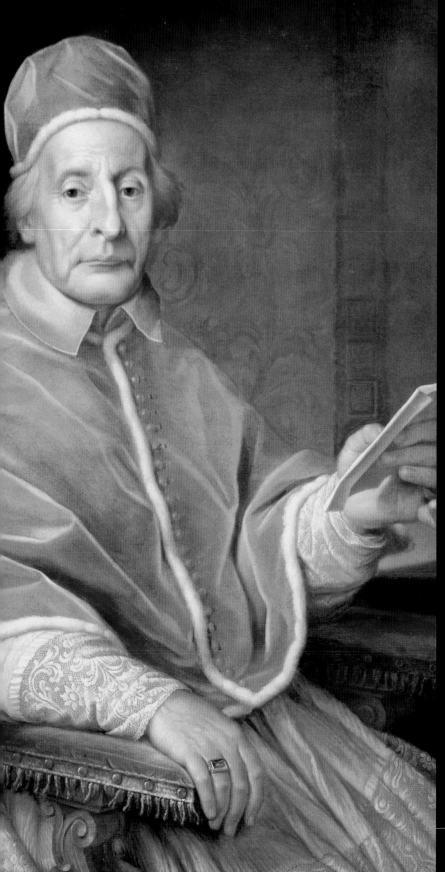

◄ Pope Clement XII who, in his papal bull of 1738, condemned Freemasonry and threatened excommunication to those who joined the Craft.

▶ Following an argument between "ancients" and "moderns," the Grand Lodge of France split, renaming itself the Grand Orient of France.

be completely independent and renamed itself the "Grand Lodge of France." Just as the formation of the United Grand Lodge of England had led to a schism within English Masonry, so the decision to reorganize the structure of French Masonry led to a split between "ancients" and "moderns." The Grand Lodge of France renamed itself the "Grand Orient of France" in 1772 and also altered its statutes, a move that led to further dissent within French Freemasonry. Perhaps predictably, some Masons refused to acknowledge these changes and continued under the original name and with the original statutes.

However, events were to take a more dramatic turn with the death of King Louis XV in 1774 and the accession to the French throne of his grandson Louis XVI. His reign was marked by a series of financial disasters and excess, which provided his own circle with wealth while the people of France experienced poverty and deprivation.

In 1788, events led Louis to hold a meeting of the Estates–General, consisting of individuals from the Church, or First Estate, the aristocracy, or Second Estate, and the middle classes, or Third Estate. The Third Estate refused to accept the influence of the other two groups and assumed the leadership of France.

The French Revolution is often seen as beginning with the storming of the Bastille, which took place on July 14th, 1789, when it was believed that Louis XVI intended to dissolve the French Assembly and challenge the power of the Third Estate. Many within the Assembly were, in fact, Freemasons. Louis was later tried for conspiring with Austrian forces and was sentenced to death. It has been estimated that as many as 320 of the total of 1,336 members of the Assembly were Freemasons. In the wake of the Revolution, many claimed that Freemasonry had been responsible for the turmoil and violence that had rocked French society.

▼ King Louis XVI intended to dissolve the French Assembly, which outraged its members, nearly one quarter of whom were Freemasons.

▲ The revolutionary cry of "Liberté, Egalité, Fraternité" is taken directly from the principles of Freemasonry.

However, Freemasonry had actually declined in popularity during the French revolution and, in many cases, lodges were suspended. Many of those involved in the initial move to revolution were Freemasons and they took their famous proclamation of "Liberty, Equality, Fraternity" from basic Masonic principles.

In many ways it is ironic that Freemasonry became associated with revolutionary activities in France, North America, and, later, Central and South America, because, according to Masonic teaching, one of the key duties of Masons is to maintain law and order and to keep their political opinions to themselves. The earliest Masonic charges or rules declare that Masons must not plot or otherwise conspire against the king or government. This principle is clearly stated in the revised con-

▶ Interestingly, and despite the apparent close similarity in the ideals of the Revolution and Freemasonry, there was a decline in membership during the Revolution.

stitutions of Dr. Anderson used by the GLE. The rift that had occurred in French Freemasonry, creating the divergent groups of Ancients and Moderns, was finally ended in 1799. They became reconciled through an Act of Union and the Grand Lodge of France became part of the Grand Orient of France.

Perhaps surprisingly, Freemasonry in France was to thrive and grow during the reign of the Emperor Napoleon Bonaparte. Initially, Napoleon regarded Freemasonry as a form of secret society and therefore a potential threat to his power, and he feared that it might shelter and nurture insurrectionary elements. He issued a decree, stating that official permission must be granted for any assembly of over 20 people, and he had investigations carried out into whether Freemasonry posed a threat to his rule. When his agents reported that Masons were not harboring any political plans against him, his suspicions were allayed and the Craft was allowed to flourish. His eventual acceptance of Freemasonry was mirrored by the close involvement of his first wife, Josephine, in a Masonic-style group. She was the Grand Mistress of the St. Caroline Lodge of adoption.

▲ Initially antagonistic toward Freemasonry, Napoleon later softened his position, perhaps owing to his wife Josephine's interest and involvement in the Craft.

## Schism with England

▼ France had always been ahead of England in the admission of women to the Craft through what was known as adoptive Freemasonry. However, when The Grand Orient of France agreed to admit atheists and agnostics, there was a major split with England, which was only healed in the early twentieth century.

During the late 1870s a major split occurred between French and English Freemasons on religious grounds. While Freemasons are drawn from a variety of religious backgrounds, it is both traditional, and according to Dr. Anderson's constitutions, a prerequisite that they express a belief in God and that a Mason will "never be a stupid atheist." The Grand Orient of France took what was perceived in England as the dramatic step of admitting atheists and agnostics into its ranks. The ritual of entry into the Brotherhood was adapted by the Grand Orient of France, and the Masonic phrase that refers to God as the Supreme Being or the Great Architect was removed. The Grand Orient of France also caused consternation among Freemasons in other countries when it declared that it would involve itself more directly in politics. But protests from abroad failed to move the governing body of French Masonry and the Grand Orient of France was declared to be irregular by other Grand Lodges. The situation was rectified only in 1913 with the formation of the National Grand Lodge of France.

MANIFESTATION DE LA FRANC-MAÇONNERIE 29 AVRIL 1871.

▶ A French nineteenth-century Masonic painting, which, although displaying much recognizable symbolism, also shows the greater inclusion of women and people from varying ethnic backgrounds.

▶ Karl Theodor, leader of the Bavarian government who in 1785 brought in a law banning all secret societies and thus declaring both Freemasons and the Illuminati to be illegal organisations.

## The Bavarian Illuminati

Freemasonry was linked to other revolutionary causes in Europe during the eighteenth century. On May 1st, 1776, a lay professor named Adam Weishaupt founded a movement that referred to itself as the "Perfectibilists," but its members became better known as the Illuminati or the "Illuminated ones." Originally the order consisted of only five members but membership reached a peak of 2,500 during its existence. It was based in Ingolstadt in Upper Bavaria. The alleged aim of the order was dramatic: to effect revolution by bringing to an end existing world governments and replacing them with a new order based on freedom and tolerance. It drew many of its members from Freemasonry but was not officially sanctioned by the Brotherhood. It had a Masonic-style structure, being organized into three primary groups that developed in seniority of position. The first stage within the Illuminati was known as Novice, the second as Minerval, while the third was designated the Minerval Illumine, or Master. Although its internal structure held obvious parallels with Freemasonry, a major distinction between the two movements was that membership of the Illuminati did not require any belief in a God or Supreme Being. A consequence of this disparity between the two groups was that many atheists were drawn to the Order. The Order became effectively illegal when the Bavarian government, led by Karl Theodor, moved to ban any form of secret society in 1785. The ban applied to Freemasons and the Illuminati alike. The adherents of the Illuminati viewed themselves as enlightened freethinkers and included artists, politicians, and writers, as well as many from aristocratic backgrounds.

▼ Ingolstadt in Upper Bavaria where, in 1776, the Illuminati movement was established and quickly flourished

# 8
# Freemasonry in America

THAT A SIGNIFICANT NUMBER OF SIGNATORIES TO BOTH THE AMERICAN DECLARATION OF INDEPENDENCE AND THE AMERICAN CONSTITUTION WERE FREEMASONS, IS A MATTER OF RECORD. BUT THE EXTENT TO WHICH FREEMASONRY EXPANDED AND ITS INFLUENCE SPREAD THROUGH THE UNITED STATES AND BEYOND, HAS ONLY RECENTLY BEEN FULLY ACKNOWLEDGED.

# Introduction

The new world of America was to prove an extremely fertile ground for Freemasonry. It has been argued that many in the old world of Europe saw in the apparently unspoiled nature of the newly discovered continent an opportunity to establish ideal utopian societies free from the mistakes of the past. Rosicrucianism and its attendant beliefs in perfecting the human soul and working toward an idealized new age of human affairs exerted a powerful influence on the development of Freemasonry. In this sense America, unfettered by the restraints of the Roman Catholic Church, presented enormous scope for the spread and influence of Freemasonic societies. Information on the early growth of Freemasonry in America is sketchy, but the movement of people and ideas from Europe clearly meant that it would be inevitable that, at some point, the Craft would be carried there.

The first known Freemason to settle in America, one whose membership of the Brotherhood is verifiable by contemporary written records, was a man called John Skene. He is thought to have been born around 1649 and his parents, Alexander Skene and Lilias Gillespie, lived in the English town of Newtyle. Skene is recorded as being a Mason within a lodge in Aberdeen

in 1670. In 1682, he emigrated to America where he settled his family on a plantation in New Jersey. Skene appears to have achieved success in his newly adopted country and rose to the rank of deputy colonial governor for West Jersey. However, lack of surviving evidence makes it seem unlikely, although not impossible,

◀ The Masonic Temple in Boston in 1865.

▶ A driving force in the struggle for independence, and a signatory to the eventual Declaration, Benjamin Franklin never sought public office.

that Skene created or participated in any Freemasonic activity in America. The first recorded settler born in America who became a Freemason was Andrew Belcher. In 1704, he was inducted into a lodge while in England. In 1733 the first American lodge to receive an official warrant from the Grand Lodge of England was St. John's Lodge of Boston. Masonic lodges were also in evidence in America within military lodges of the British Army that conducted their ceremonies and meetings in the field. Benjamin Franklin played a major role in the promotion of Freemasonry in America through his work in newspapers such as the *Pennsylvania Gazette*. Franklin became a Mason in 1732 and became Junior Warden of the Pennsylvania Grand Lodge in the same year. It has been argued that the lodge system in America provided a forum for the discussion of views at this time and also served to a great extent as a unifying factor for the colonies. Franklin became an outspoken defender of American rights against the controls of the British government and he would, of course, play a major role in the foundation of the emerging nation.

# Boston Tea Party

The Boston Tea Party is today remembered as one of the most important events leading to the American Revolution and the achievement of independence from British rule. American Freemasons were directly involved in this symbolic act of defiance. A small party of men, who had concealed their identities by dressing as Mohawk tribesmen, stole aboard a British merchant ship, the *Dartmouth*, on December 16th, 1773. The ship was the property of the British East India Company. Once on board the men proceeded to throw its load of 32 chests of tea into Boston's harbor. The value of the tea was estimated at 10,000 pounds. The purpose of this seemingly bizarre act of sabotage was to protest against taxation on tea and, more generally, against British taxation without democratic representation. It is claimed that the raid was formulated in the "Long Room" of Freemasons' Hall, an establishment that had previously been the Green Dragon tavern. The group that carried out the raid was known as the "Sons of Liberty," but Freemasons were among their number. Twelve members of St. Andrew's Lodge, Boston, participated in the Tea Party. It is worthy of note that a further 12 later became Freemasons following this act of subversion.

▶ "No taxation without representation" was a phrase that would resonate around the world long after the so-called Boston Tea Party in which men dressed as Native Americans threw a cargo of tea overboard. Many of them were Freemasons.

# The American Revolution

George Washington led the largely untrained colonial army against the British forces.

▼ George Washington led the Colonial army against British forces and then left the army to become his country's first president. Here he is shown with French General Jean de Rochambeau ,just before the battle of Yorktown.

George Washington led the largely untrained colonial army against the British forces. Washington was born in Virginia in 1732 and had been made a Freemason in 1753 when he was initiated into the Fredericksburg lodge. In 1788, he became the charter master of a lodge in Alexandria. However, although Washington, like

many of the generals of the colonial army, was a Mason, it appears that he was not particularly closely involved in lodge activities. While Washington led the conflict, Franklin traveled to France to seek aid. In 1777, he was initiated into the Lodge des Neuf Soeurs, or the Lodge of the Nine Sisters, in Paris. The following year he helped initiate Voltaire into the lodge. The friendship between the two men helped sway the sympathy of the French people toward the American cause.

There were Freemasons on both sides at the time of the American Revolution. An interesting and unusual example of a Native American becoming a Freemason is the Mohawk war leader Joseph Brant, known as Thayendanegea in his own language. Brant visited Britain in 1775 to represent the Mohawk people, who were fighting on the side of the British, and to ensure that the British Crown and its officials would make good their promises of protection when the conflict ceased. During the 1770s, Brant had risen to the rank of captain in the British army. When he came to England he was inducted into a Masonic lodge and mixed with a number of notable figures from English society, including James Boswell and Hugh Percy, Second Duke of Northumberland. Today, the Masonic apron given to him by the lodge is held at Barton Lodge in Hamilton, Ontario. Upon Brant's return to America he was involved in fighting with the rebels and the British later handed over prisoners to the Mohawk for torture. It is reported that when a number of prisoners made Masonic signs Brant had them freed.

▲ Washington was a Freemason for most of his adult life, although he was not as actively involved in lodge matters as Benjamin Franklin.

◄ While in France, Franklin, already a member, initiated Voltaire into the Lodge des Neuf Soeurs in Paris.

# The American Declaration of Independence

When the Declaration of Independence was published by Congress in 1776, 15 of the 56 signers were Freemasons or likely to have been members. It has been argued that the ideals and values of Freemasonry also exerted a powerful influence over the

▲ Of the 56 signatories to the Declaration of independence, 15 were known to be Freemasons.

formulation of the American Constitution, confirmed on September 13th, 1788. It is known that 28 of the 40 signers of this document were either known to be Masons or likely to have been members of the Brotherhood.

George Washington and Benjamin Franklin were known Masons, as were John Blair, John Dickinson, Rufus King, Gunning Bedford Junior, David Brearly, Daniel Carroll, and Jacob Broom. Interestingly, a further number of the signers of the Constitution became Freemasons at a later date. George Washington was elected as the first president of the United States of America on February 4th, 1789.

◄ Benjamin Franklin and others present the signed Declaration of Independence, clearly aware of their momentous decision, the effects of which continue to be felt around the world today.

# IN CONGRESS, JULY 4, 1776.

# The unanimous Declaration of the thirteen united States of America.

When in the Course of human events, it becomes necessary for one people to dissolve the political bands which have connected them with another, and to assume among the powers of the earth, the separate and equal station to which the Laws of Nature and of Nature's God entitle them, a decent respect to the opinions of mankind requires that they should declare the causes which impel them to the separation.

We hold these truths to be self-evident, that all men are created equal, that they are endowed by their Creator with certain unalienable Rights, that among these are Life, Liberty and the pursuit of Happiness.—That to secure these rights, Governments are instituted among Men, deriving their just powers from the consent of the governed,—That whenever any Form of Government becomes destructive of these ends, it is the Right of the People to alter or to abolish it, and to institute new Government, laying its foundation on such principles and organizing its powers in such form, as to them shall seem most likely to effect their Safety and Happiness. Prudence, indeed, will dictate that Governments long established should not be changed for light and transient causes; and accordingly all experience hath shewn, that mankind are more disposed to suffer, while evils are sufferable, than to right themselves by abolishing the forms to which they are accustomed. But when a long train of abuses and usurpations, pursuing invariably the same Object evinces a design to reduce them under absolute Despotism, it is their right, it is their duty, to throw off such Government, and to provide new Guards for their future security.—Such has been the patient sufferance of these Colonies; and such is now the necessity which constrains them to alter their former Systems of Government. The history of the present King of Great Britain is a history of repeated injuries and usurpations, all having in direct object the establishment of an absolute Tyranny over these States. To prove this, let Facts be submitted to a candid world.

He has refused his Assent to Laws, the most wholesome and necessary for the public good.

He has forbidden his Governors to pass Laws of immediate and pressing importance, unless suspended in their operation till his Assent should be obtained; and when so suspended, he has utterly neglected to attend to them.

He has refused to pass other Laws for the accommodation of large districts of people, unless those people would relinquish the right of Representation in the Legislature, a right inestimable to them and formidable to tyrants only.

He has called together legislative bodies at places unusual, uncomfortable, and distant from the depository of their Public Records, for the sole purpose of fatiguing them into compliance with his measures.

He has dissolved Representative Houses repeatedly, for opposing with manly firmness his invasions on the rights of the people.

He has refused for a long time, after such dissolutions, to cause others to be elected; whereby the Legislative powers, incapable of Annihilation, have returned to the People at large for their exercise; the State remaining in the mean time exposed to all the dangers of invasion from without, and convulsions within.

He has endeavoured to prevent the population of these States; for that purpose obstructing the Laws for Naturalization of Foreigners; refusing to pass others to encourage their migrations hither, and raising the conditions of new Appropriations of Lands.

He has obstructed the Administration of Justice, by refusing his Assent to Laws for establishing Judiciary powers.

He has made Judges dependent on his Will alone, for the tenure of their offices, and the amount and payment of their salaries.

He has erected a multitude of New Offices, and sent hither swarms of Officers to harrass our people, and eat out their substance.

He has kept among us, in times of peace, Standing Armies without the Consent of our legislatures.

He has affected to render the Military independent of and superior to the Civil power.

He has combined with others to subject us to a jurisdiction foreign to our constitution, and unacknowledged by our laws; giving his Assent to their Acts of pretended Legislation:

For Quartering large bodies of armed troops among us:

For protecting them, by a mock Trial, from punishment for any Murders which they should commit on the Inhabitants of these States:

For cutting off our Trade with all parts of the world:

For imposing Taxes on us without our Consent:

For depriving us in many cases, of the benefits of Trial by Jury:

For transporting us beyond Seas to be tried for pretended offences

For abolishing the free System of English Laws in a neighbouring Province, establishing therein an Arbitrary government, and enlarging its Boundaries so as to render it at once an example and fit instrument for introducing the same absolute rule into these Colonies:

For taking away our Charters, abolishing our most valuable Laws, and altering fundamentally the Forms of our Governments:

For suspending our own Legislatures, and declaring themselves invested with power to legislate for us in all cases whatsoever.

He has abdicated Government here, by declaring us out of his Protection and waging War against us.

He has plundered our seas, ravaged our Coasts, burnt our towns, and destroyed the lives of our people.

He is at this time transporting large Armies of foreign Mercenaries to compleat the works of death, desolation and tyranny, already begun with circumstances of Cruelty & perfidy scarcely paralleled in the most barbarous ages, and totally unworthy the Head of a civilized nation.

He has constrained our fellow Citizens taken Captive on the high Seas to bear Arms against their Country, to become the executioners of their friends and Brethren, or to fall themselves by their Hands.

He has excited domestic insurrections amongst us, and has endeavoured to bring on the inhabitants of our frontiers, the merciless Indian Savages, whose known rule of warfare, is an undistinguished destruction of all ages, sexes and conditions.

In every stage of these Oppressions We have Petitioned for Redress in the most humble terms: Our repeated Petitions have been answered only by repeated injury. A Prince, whose character is thus marked by every act which may define a Tyrant, is unfit to be the ruler of a free people.

Nor have We been wanting in attentions to our British brethren. We have warned them from time to time of attempts by their legislature to extend an unwarrantable jurisdiction over us. We have reminded them of the circumstances of our emigration and settlement here. We have appealed to their native justice and magnanimity, and we have conjured them by the ties of our common kindred to disavow these usurpations, which, would inevitably interrupt our connections and correspondence. They too have been deaf to the voice of justice and of consanguinity. We must, therefore, acquiesce in the necessity, which denounces our Separation, and hold them, as we hold the rest of mankind, Enemies in War, in Peace Friends.

We, therefore, the Representatives of the united States of America, in General Congress, Assembled, appealing to the Supreme Judge of the world for the rectitude of our intentions, do, in the Name, and by Authority of the good People of these Colonies, solemnly publish and declare, That these United Colonies are, and of Right ought to be Free and Independent States; that they are Absolved from all Allegiance to the British Crown, and that all political connection between them and the State of Great Britain, is and ought to be totally dissolved; and that as Free and Independent States, they have full Power to levy War, conclude Peace, contract Alliances, establish Commerce, and to do all other Acts and Things which Independent States may of right do.—And for the support of this Declaration, with a firm reliance on the protection of divine Providence, we mutually pledge to each other our Lives, our Fortunes and our sacred Honor.

John Hancock

Button Gwinnett
Lyman Hall
Geo Walton

Wm Hooper
Joseph Hewes
John Penn

Edward Rutledge
Thos Heyward Junr.
Thomas Lynch Junr.
Arthur Middleton

Samuel Chase
Wm Paca
Thos Stone
Charles Carroll of Carrollton

George Wythe
Richard Henry Lee
Th Jefferson
Benja Harrison
Thos Nelson jr.
Francis Lightfoot Lee
Carter Braxton

Robt Morris
Benjamin Rush
Benja Franklin
John Morton
Geo Clymer
Jas Smith
Geo Taylor
James Wilson
Geo Ross
Caesar Rodney
Geo Read
Tho McKean

Wm Floyd
Phil. Livingston
Frans Lewis
Lewis Morris
Richd Stockton
Jno Witherspoon
Fras Hopkinson
John Hart
Abra Clark

Josiah Bartlett
Wm Whipple
Saml Adams
John Adams
Robt Treat Paine
Elbridge Gerry
Step Hopkins
William Ellery
Roger Sherman
Samel Huntington
Wm Williams
Oliver Wolcott
Matthew Thornton

When Washington took the presidential oath of office on April 30th, 1789, the ceremony was administered by Robert Livingstone, the Grand Master of New York's Grand Lodge. Benjamin Franklin died on April 17th, 1789, and did not live to see Washington's presidential inauguration. Freemasons also played a major role when Washington laid the cornerstone of the Capitol on September 18th, 1793. A great procession was held, which included the Grand Lodge of Maryland, with Washington acting as its Master, together with members of his own lodge from Alexandria, Virginia. The Grand Lodge of Maryland was accompanied by other affiliated lodges.

◀ The Declaration of Independence, signed on 4th July, 1776.

◀ George Washington taking the presidential oath of office on February 4th, 1789.

## A New Cornerstone

A silver plate, carrying the designations of the lodges present, had been specially made for the occasion. After a ceremonial volley had been fired into the air Washington stepped down into a trench in which the south-east cornerstone was set. He put the commemorative silver plate on top of the stone. He also set offerings of corn, oil, and wine in jars in the trench, all important symbols within Masonic rituals. The assembled gathering of Freemasons offered prayers, which were followed by a second volley of shots into the air.

▼ The capitol building in Washington, the seat of government of the United States of America, is constructed according to Masonic geometrical principles, as is the whole city.

After he had laid the offerings in the trench, Washington ascended a small rostrum with the three steps common to Masonic ritual and addressed the assembly. Michael Baigent and Richard Leigh, in their book *The Temple and the Lodge*, contend that the White House and the Capitol formed the basis of a geometrical design for the city of Washington that has Masonic significance. They argue that George Washington and Thomas Jefferson planned them as the focal centers of octagonal patterns whose shape incorporates the specific cross that Masonic Templars use in their symbolism.

▶ (Next spread) An 18th century mural which shows George Washington, first President of the United States of America laying the cornerstone of the US Capitol building dressed in full Masonic regalia.

## Washington House of the Temple

An important Masonic landmark within the capital city of Washington is the House of the Temple. This temple serves as the headquarters of the Supreme Council, 33 degrees, Ancient and Accepted Scottish Rite of Freemasonry, Southern Jurisdiction of America. The corner-stone of the building was put in place on October 18th, 1911, and the ceremony of dedication marking its completion took place on October 18th, 1915. The temple is also the final resting place of the Civil War general Albert Pike, who was hugely influential in popular-izing the Scottish Rite within the Southern Jurisdiction of American Freemasonry. The architecture of the House of the Temple was based on the Mausoleum of Mausolos, one of the Seven Wonders of the Ancient World.

▶ The architecture of the House of the Temple in Washington was based on the Mausoleum of Mausolos, one of the Seven Wonders of the Ancient World.

## Prince Hall Freemasonry

The first African-American to become a Freemason was a man called Prince Hall, who was initiated into the Irish Constitution Military Lodge in Boston Massachusetts in 1775. Prince Hall became a Freemason with 14 other "freeborn" African–Americans. Although few details have survived about the life of Prince Hall, some claim that he was born on September 12th, 1748, in Barbados. He may have been a slave in Boston and may have been freed in 1770. He is believed to have fought in the Revolutionary War. After being initiated as Freemasons, Prince Hall and the 14 other African–American men who had also become Masons applied for a Lodge Warrant from the Premier Grand Lodge of England. Their application was successful and they went on to form African Lodge, Number 459 (Premier Grand Lodge of England) in 1787.

Under the conditions of the Premier Grand Lodge of England, the newly established African Lodge was able to give permission for the foundation of other lodges with itself as the head lodge. Subsequently, further African Lodges came into being in other American cities, such as New York. In 1791, Prince Hall became the Grand Master of the African Grand Lodge of North America and, following his death in 1807, the name of the lodge was changed in 1808 to the Prince Hall Grand Lodge of Massachusetts as a tribute to him. During his life Hall was active in promoting the foundation of schools for black children from Boston. The African Lodge of Boston became independent from the Grand Lodge of England in 1827. It is recognized that the African–American Prince Hall Freemasons contributed greatly to the education of black men and women both within their lodges and also by providing funds for college scholarships. Today, Prince Hall lodges, like most Masonic lodges, are open to those from a multi-ethnic background.

▲ Prince Hall, the first African-American to become a Freemason. He rose to the office of Grand Master of the African Grand Lodge of North America, which was later renamed in his honor,.

# The Scottish Rite

Freemasonry was to flourish in America and two further systems of Masonic degrees have been adopted to allow Master Masons to learn more about the Craft. For those who have achieved the first three stages of Blue Lodge Masonic development, Entered Apprentice, Fellowcraft, and Master Mason, the Scottish Rite offers an opportunity for candidates to progress within a framework of a further 30 degrees. However, the final degree, the thirty-third degree, cannot be applied for by individuals but is bestowed on Masons who are thought to have made a particularly significant contribution to the world of Freemasonry or the Scottish Rite in particular, or who are deemed to have performed some exceptional service to humanity. The Scottish Rite is recognized by American Grand Lodges as an extension of the traditional three degrees. In England it is not officially recognized by the Grand Lodge, but Freemasons are not prevented from undertaking it.

▼ Albert Pike, who is associated with the popular spread of the Scottish Rite within the Southern Jurisdiction of America.

There has been considerable speculation about the development of the Scottish Rite. It has been suggested by Michael Baigent and Richard Leigh and other commentators that this particular branch of Freemasonry was influenced by and inseparably linked to the Jacobite cause of the seventeenth and eighteenth centuries. In America the Scottish Rite proved to be an outstanding success and, in South Carolina, the Supreme Council of the Ancient and Accepted Scottish Rite was established in 1801, the first such council of the Scottish Rite to be founded. The popularity and success of the Scottish Rite within the history of the Southern Jurisdiction of American Freemasonry is very often attributed to Albert Pike.

Pike was born in Boston, Massachusetts, on December 29th, 1809. He received the fourth to thirty-second degrees in Charleston in 1853, and the thirty-third in 1857 in New Orleans.

Today the Scottish Rite within America is governed by two Supreme Councils. The Supreme Council of the Southern Jurisdiction is based in Washington, D.C., while the Supreme Council of the Northern Masonic Jurisdiction is located in Lexington, Massachusetts. Masons working through the different degrees of the Scottish Rite meet in groups known as "Valleys," over which the Supreme Council has particular authority.

▼ The House of the Temple in Washington was completed in 1915 and is the headquarters for the Supreme Council of the Southern Jurisdiction.

In all there are a further 30 degrees through which a mason has to pass before attaining the highest degree of Knight Commander of the Court of Honor. According to the various Scottish Rite jurisdictions in the world, all of which operate independently, the Scottish Rite degrees are worked at will by their governing bodies. For example, the Southern Jurisdiction separates the degrees as follows:

• Fourth through fourteenth degree: Lodge of Perfection
• Fifteenth through eighteenth degree: Chapter of Rose Croix
• Nineteenth through thirtieth degree: Council of Kadosh
• Thirty-first and thirty-third degree: Consistory

This is different in the Northern Jurisdiction:
• Fourth through fourteenth degree: Lodge of Perfection
• Fifteenth and sixteenth degree: Council of Prince of Jerusalem
• Seventeenth and eighteenth degree: Chapter of Rose Croix
• Nineteenth through thirty-third degree: Consistory

▶ The façade of the Scottish Rite Masonic Center in McAlester, Oklahoma, which is considered to be one of the most imposing temples in North America.

# The York Rite

The York Rite also offers an opportunity for Master Masons to progress further within the world of Freemasonry beyond the standard three degrees of Blue Lodge Masonry. It is found mainly as a single system in America and there are differences within the different Orders that teach it. There are three stages within the York Rite:

## Royal Arch Masonry

The order known as Royal Arch Masonry, also referred to as the Chapter, indicates a group of Royal Arch Masons. Within Royal Arch Masonry candidates may undertake the Mark Master Mason degree. It takes its name and symbolism from the practice of medieval masons carving individual symbols upon the structures and stonework for which they were responsible in order that they might be recognized by other masons.

The next degree within Royal Arch Masonry is that of Virtual Past Master. This is followed by the degree of Most Excellent Master and is unique within Freemasonry in that its imagery is of the completion of King Solomon's Temple.

The final degree in the sequence is that of the Royal Arch Mason. This is often termed the "most beautiful," sublime, or elegant degree within Freemasonry.

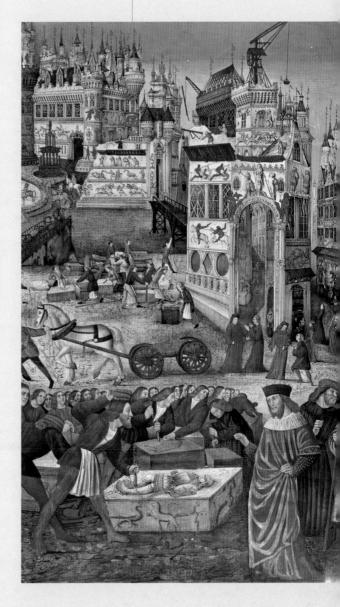

▼ The stages of the York Rite have a strong symbolic link with the building of the Temple of Solomon, particularly during the stage known as Royal Arch Masonry.

## Cryptic Masonry

Those who reach this elevated Masonic degree are eligible, but not obliged, to undertake the degrees of Cryptic Masonry. The degrees within the Cryptic Rite are that of Royal Master, Select Master, and Super Excellent Master. It derives this secondary term of identification because some form of underground chamber or crypt-like room forms a part of the developing degrees that it encompasses.

## The Commandery of Knights Templar

The third and final body within the York Rite is known as the Commandery of Knights Templar. It is unusual in Masonic groups in that its membership does require a specific religious belief system. While Freemasonry in general is open to individuals with a belief in a supreme being, the degree of Knights Templar is open only to Master Masons whose religion is Christianity.

▼ The stages of the York Rite have a strong symbolic link with the building of the Temple of Solomon, particularly during the stage known as Royal Arch Masonry.

# William Morgan

Freemasonry had grown exponentially in America but it was dealt a major blow in 1826 with the mysterious case of the disappearance of a man called William Morgan. He was from Culpepper County in Virginia and had traveled to Canada to find work, eventually taking up residence in the town of Batavia in New York State. Records show that Morgan was awarded the Royal Arch degree in the Western Star Chapter No. 33 of Le Roy on May 31st, 1825. Sources differ as to how he became involved in Freemasonry and some within the Brotherhood allege deception and dishonesty. Morgan was among a group of Freemasons from Batavia who sought permission to establish a Royal Arch chapter. Although they were successful in their aim, Morgan himself was later rejected by his fellow Masons. This rejection led him to attack the Order, claiming that he had written a book that would expose important Masonic secrets to the general public. He also claimed that he had signed a contract for the publication of this book, which would expose the inner workings of Freemasonry, and would involve a payment to him of the huge figure of $500,000.

The publishers of the book were said to include David C. Miller who, like Morgan, was a disgruntled Freemason, and two others. Morgan was reportedly extremely vocal about the book and caused considerable consternation within the Brotherhood. Events took a sinister turn when he was arrested in

▼ There was a strong backlash against Freemasonry following the William Morgan case, typified by the leaflet shown here.

▶ Satirists became increasingly vitriolic, lampooning some of the most senior members of the government who were also Freemasons.

ALL ON HOBBIES, GEE UP, GEE HO.!

September 1826 for a dubious and unlikely minor offence; he was alleged to have stolen a shirt and tie. Although the charge came to nothing he was actually jailed for having failed to pay an outstanding debt of a few dollars. Morgan was to spend only a single day in jail, as a mysterious and still unknown benefactor settled the amount he owed. However, as soon as he was released, it was reported that a small group of men forced him to accompany them away from the jail in a coach. The men allegedly took him to a disused fort where they detained him.

The news of the apparent abduction of William Morgan led to feverish speculation that he had been taken by Freemasons who had killed him to prevent their secrets being revealed. When a body was discovered on the banks of the river Niagara it was at first thought that it must be that of the kidnapped Morgan. The corpse was initially identified as Morgan by his own wife because it was wearing his clothes. On closer inspection the identification was questioned because marks and scars on the body did not match those known to be on Morgan's body. After three separate inquests, it was established that the body actually belonged to a Canadian, Timothy Munro, who was identified by his wife, Sara.

The mystery of the fate of William Morgan had meanwhile remained unresolved. Seven men, all known to be Masons, were subsequently arrested for the kidnapping of Morgan but charges of murder were never made because of the absence of an identifiable body. The fate of the abducted man has never been conclusively proved but, at the time, the news of his alleged abduction by a band of Freemasons trying to prevent the secret workings of their Order being made public, sent shock waves of fear across America. Suddenly Freemasons were regarded as a sinister and evil force at work within American society. In the immediate aftermath of the kidnapping anti-Masonic feelings ran high. The Church condemned Masons, individuals were forced out of their jobs for being Masons, newspapers such as the *Anti-Masonic Review* were founded, and there was a significant decrease in the number of Masonic candidates and Lodges across America.

◀ Thurlow Weed was an influential backer of political candidates and a strong opponent of Freemasonry. While campaigning he used William Morgan's disappearance to discredit Masonic members of the United States government.

# 9
# Freemasonry in the Modern Era

AS FREEMASONRY BECAME LESS SECRETIVE ABOUT ITS ACTIVITIES, THE EXTENT TO WHICH ITS REACH INTO MANY AREAS BECAME APPARENT, CREATING AN ALMOST INEVITABLE BACKLASH OF ACCUSATIONS AND CONSPIRACY THEORIES.

# Introduction

While a diverse and famous range of individuals, including such figures as Winston Churchill, Oscar Wilde, and John Wayne, have been Freemasons, the public image of the Craft in the modern era has very often been a negative one. Conspiracy theories implicating Masonry in plans for world domination have abounded and Freemasons have very often found themselves at the receiving end of bigotry and intolerance.

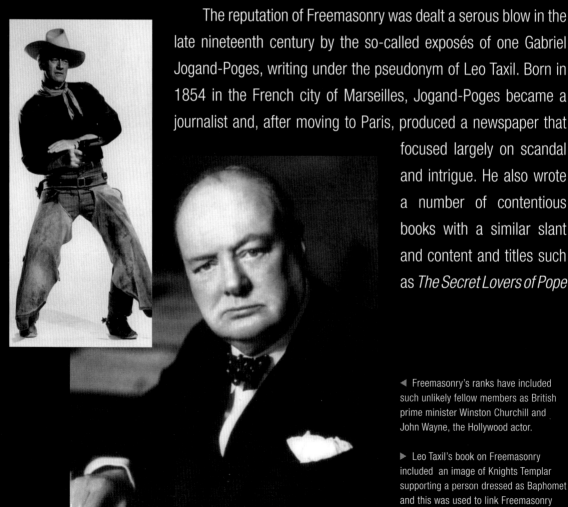

The reputation of Freemasonry was dealt a serous blow in the late nineteenth century by the so-called exposés of one Gabriel Jogand-Poges, writing under the pseudonym of Leo Taxil. Born in 1854 in the French city of Marseilles, Jogand-Poges became a journalist and, after moving to Paris, produced a newspaper that focused largely on scandal and intrigue. He also wrote a number of contentious books with a similar slant and content and titles such as *The Secret Lovers of Pope*

◄ Freemasonry's ranks have included such unlikely fellow members as British prime minister Winston Churchill and John Wayne, the Hollywood actor.

▶ Leo Taxil's book on Freemasonry included  an image of Knights Templar supporting a person dressed as Baphomet and this was used to link Freemasonry with pagan practices.

*Pius IX*. He became a Freemason in 1881 but was eventually rejected by the Brotherhood. Subsequently Jogand-Poges adopted Catholicism and, perhaps inspired by the Catholic hatred of Freemasonry, wrote a number of books exposing the secrets of Masonry. Entitled *The Secret Revelations of French Masonry*, the books portrayed Freemasons as satanic devil worshipers who engaged in the most appalling and debased behavior during their rites and rituals.

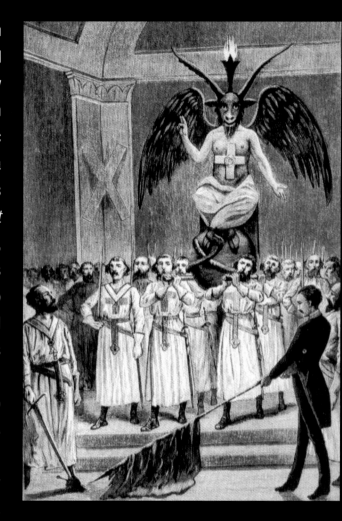

The books of Leo Taxil were to prove an incredible popular success throughout Europe. His works on Freemasonry were also particularly anti-Semitic in their content and his vivid descriptions of Masonic secret ceremonies were fantastical and demonic. Taxil insisted that the punishment for Masons who betrayed the secrets of the Brotherhood was, potentially, death, and that all Masons, as part of their oath or charge of allegiance, must be ready to commit murder. While many within Freemasonry objected publicly to his distortion of the image of the Brotherhood, he was, perhaps not surprisingly, supported in his attack on the Craft by the Catholic Church. The pope of the day, Leo XIII, went so far as to award Leo Taxil the special honor of the Order of the Holy Sepulcher as a reward for his attacks on Freemasonry.

# Women in Freemasonry

Although Freemasonry has traditionally been dominated by men, there are Masonic bodies that are open to women. An interesting example of a woman being admitted to a Masonic lodge at a time when Masonry was essentially a male-only affair is the case of Elizabeth St. Leger. It is said that, in 1713, Elizabeth had witnessed a lodge meeting in session at the house of her father who

▲ A German Freemason holds up a compass and square during a meeting in Göttingen in 2007.

was First Viscount Doneraile in the Irish county of Cork. Although it might seem unusual for a lodge meeting to have taken place in her father's house, it seems to have been normal at that time, and the lodge in question had a warrant from the Grand Lodge of Ireland. It is said that she took a brick from an internal wall and was able to see into the room where the lodge was meeting. Her presence was detected and it was decided that the best course of action was to make her a Mason. She was active within Masonry during her life and was apparently treated as an equal within the fraternity. Upon her death, she is said to have received full Masonic honors at her funeral.

◄ Adoptive Freemasonry grew in France in the post-revolutionary period, as depicted in this initiation ceremony for a female Freemason to the Grand Orient of France in the nineteenth century, by which time female membership was universal.

However, the admission of women into Freemasonry did not occur widely until 1882, when Maria Deraismes became a Mason, joining the Loge Libres Penseurs, or "Freethinkers Lodge," in France. This lodge was under the jurisdiction of the Grand Independent Symbolic Lodge and had broken away from the Supreme Council of France. When the Grand Lodge discovered this, they suspended Les Libres Penseurs. However, in 1892, Maria Deraismes was approached by a member of the Supreme Council, Dr. Georges Martin, who suggested that they found a lodge that would be open to both men and women. They established a lodge called Le Droit Humain, or "the Human Duty," and initiated 16 women into its ranks together with male Masons. Over the course of the next few years its popularity grew and, in 1907, the Order extended the three degrees that it had offered to include the 33 degrees of the Ancient and Accepted Scottish Rite.

▼ Annie Besant, a leading member of the Theosophical Society and mentor of the spiritual teacher J. Krishnamurti successfully established mixed Masonry in England.

In Britain, the concept of mixed Masonry was, arguably, most successfully established by Annie Besant of the Theosophical Society. Members of the Theosophical Society were also drawn to the idea of what was initially known as "Joint Freemasonry" and later as "Universal Co-Freemasonry." Le Droit Humain and the Order of International Co-Masonry are still in existence today. However, the United Grand Lodge of England, while recognizing and acknowledging orders of mixed Masonry, does not allow women to become members of its particular Masonic order.

In the United States of America, the Order of the Eastern Star was formed in 1850 and its members were, and are, drawn mainly from Masons and the female relatives of Master Masons. The Order of the Eastern Star was founded by Dr. Robert Morris, himself a former Grand Master of Kentucky. Initially,

Dr. Morris had planned to develop a form of women's Freemasonry, but the idea proved so unpopular amongst male Masons that the compromise position of mixed Masonry was adopted. The headquarters of the Order is in Washington, D.C., and housed in the Eastern Star Temple. In order to be eligible for membership a woman must currently be over the age of 18 and be the wife, daughter, widow, sister, half-sister, mother, stepmother, granddaughter, niece, or grandmother of a Master Mason.

An interesting variation on Freemasonry is the Order of Weavers, a women's group that has Masonic links but, rather than basing its moral and philosophical lessons and rituals on symbols drawn from stonemasonry, it makes use of ideas and images that derive from the practice of weaving.

▲ A symbol of the Rosicrucian order.

▼ Samuel Liddel McGregor, one of the three founding members of the Golden Dawn.

# The Golden Dawn

Freemasonry, along with Rosicrucian thought and the influence of the Theosophical Society, was to play an important role in the emergence of the magical order known as the Golden Dawn. Founded in 1887, the order was secretive in nature and consisted of both male and female members. The order began with three founding members, William Wynn Westcott, Samuel Liddell MacGregor, and Dr. William Robert Woodman. All three were Freemasons and were also linked to the Masonic-style group Societas Rosicruciana in Anglia, or the SRIA. As is the case with Freemasonry, the Golden Dawn was organized around a system of degrees of ascending initiation. Within the order of the Golden Dawn there were 14 different degrees. The order was strongly influenced by Hermetic thought and its members were instructed in alchemy and the Kabbalistic tradition, among other subjects.

The members of the Golden Dawn believed that they constituted an elite and developed an elaborate system of personal development, reflected in the fact that their training featured so many degrees of initiation. While Freemasonry was a movement that was well known within its respective societies, or, some might argue, at least maintained a public image that was widely recognized within those societies, knowledge of the existence of the order of the Golden Dawn was limited. Its most famous members included Aleister Crowley, W.B. Yeats, and Dion Fortune.

◄ ▲ Dr William Robert Woodman,
a founder member of the Golden
Dawn, and the Irish poet W.B.
Yeats, who became an enthusiastic
member of the order.

# The Holocaust

It has been estimated that as many as 80,000 to 200,000 Freemasons were killed by the Nazi regime during the Second World War. In *Mein Kampf* Hitler declared that Freemasonry had "succumbed" to the Jews. He argued further that Freemasonry represented an "excellent instrument" for the Jews to manipulate and shape society. For Hitler the "general pacifist paralysis of the national instinct of self-preservation" of Germany following the First World War was directly attributable to Freemasonry.

▲ The title page of Mein Kampf in which Adolf Hitler laid out his thoughts and prejudices on a variety of subjects and peoples, including Freemasonry ,which he accused, along with the Jewish people, of manipulating society.

▶ Senior Nazi officers on a tour of an exhibition set up as propaganda against Jews and other groups, including Freemasons, held in Munich in 1937, here stand under a Masonic symbol.

It is a little known fact that the famous American industrialist, Henry Ford, best known for the production of automobiles, was strongly anti-Semitic and also viewed the Freemasons as being part of a Jewish conspiracy to control the United States of America. Ford gave his own personal stamp of approval to a 1922 edition of an anti-Semitic piece of propaganda, *The Protocols of the Elders of Zion*, by writing an introduction to it. He also aired his prejudices in the *Dearborn Independent*, his own weekly journal. He used it as a platform to publish a long series of splenetic, paranoid outbursts against Jews and their influence in America. While the titles of Ford's diatribes, ranging from "Jewish Gamblers Corrupt American Baseball" to "Jewish Jazz Becomes our National Music," may have seemed almost comically hysterical, their content was unrelentingly sinister and filled with hatred.

Such was the scale of the obsessive outpourings from his journal on the subject that he finally had the articles compiled into a book form with the repugnant title of *The International Jew: The World's Foremost Problem*. The book became a bestseller both in America and abroad. It comes as little surprise to discover that it was greeted with great personal enthusiasm by Adolf Hitler himself. Such was Hitler's regard for Henry Ford that he is said to have kept a picture of him in his office. Ford would argue that the role of the Freemasons in America was in fact to shift attention away from the labyrinthine anti-American plots of the Jews. He later apologized publicly for his anti-Semitic outpourings, although it seems unlikely he felt any genuine regret about them.

▲ The industrialist Henry Ford wrote an introduction to a piece of anti-Semitic piece propaganda published in America in 1922 and later made into a book, which also criticized Freemasonry ,and for which he later apologized publicly.

# The P2 Scandal

Perhaps the greatest scandal relating to Freemasonry in the twentieth century centered on the Italian Masonic lodge P2 and the murder of Roberto Calvi. Formed in 1895 under the jurisdiction of the Grand Orient of Italy, P2 became increasingly corrupt, particularly under Grand Master Licio Gelli. P2 was actually dissolved as a Masonic lodge in Italy and Gelli was thrown out of Freemasonry in 1976. However, he continued to operate the P2 lodge, largely as a front for criminal dealings. P2 became front-page news when, in 1982, the president of Banco Ambrosiano, Roberto Calvi, was murdered and found hanging under Blackfriars Bridge in London. He had disappeared shortly beforehand just as he had been about to give evidence in court regarding the involvement of P2 with Banco Ambrosiano and the Vatican. Originally his death was described as suicide but subsequent investigations established that he had, in fact, been murdered.

◄ Italian banker Roberto Calvi, who was found hanged in London in 1982.

# Conspiracy Theories

In recent years Freemasons have become far more open about their activities and their rituals, but in the past this was not the case and theories abounded about the involvement of Freemasons in unsavory activities. An example of this, which continues to attract such theories, are the horrific murders carried out by Jack the Ripper in Victorian London. These have been linked to amongst others the Queen's doctor, Sir William Gull. It was claimed by Joseph Sickert, son of the painter Walter Sickert, that Sir William was involved and that his fellow Masons were obliged to protect him. The nature of the killings is supposed to have reflected Masonic rituals.

However, the credibility of the story is undermined by reports that Sickert later admitted that the story had been a fiction. Critics of the theory have also argued that it seems unlikely that Gull would have been physically capable of carrying out the killings. Aged 72, the doctor had already experienced a heart attack. It seems more likely that the identity of Jack the Ripper has never been unequivocally established because police methods of the time were inadequate for dealing with serial killings of this nature.

The death of the Austrian composer Wolfgang Amadeus Mozart,

▼ Endless theories have been put forward about the identity of Jack the Ripper, with the Freemasonry connection being one of the most popular and persistent.

▼ A US dollar bill, the design of which is rich in Masonic symbolism.

himself a Mason, in mysterious circumstances has also led to theories implicating the Freemasons. *The Magic Flute* features Masonic themes and subject matter and it is suggested that he produced the opera as a piece of pro-Masonic propaganda to celebrate the coronation of Leopold II as Austrian Emperor in 1791. The events of the French and American Revolutions had badly tarnished the image of Freemasonry and it was hoped to influence the new ruler by showing the Craft in a positive light.

When Mozart died on December 5th, 1791, it was rumored that he had been poisoned. No autopsy was carried out on his body and theories soon began to circulate about the nature of his death and the possible reasons behind it. One version of events claimed that Mozart had been murdered for revealing Masonic secrets in *The Magic Flute* or that he had been a sacrifice to so-called Masonic deities. However, in a posthumous investigation held into the circumstances of his death in 2000, a group of physicians concluded that the composer had, in fact, died as a result of rheumatic fever.

More recently, Freemasonry has featured strongly in a variety of conspiracy theories concerning modern American society. It has been argued that the influence of Freemasonry can be found amongst some of the most visible symbols of the United States of America. Attention has focused on the Great Seal of the United States, which commonly

appears in official contexts and on government documents. On the reverse side of the Great Seal a pyramid with 13 steps, surmounted by the "Eye of Providence," is depicted. Within Masonic symbolism, the floating, disembodied eye is representative of God, who is often referred to as the "Great Architect." The eye on the Great Seal is surrounded by a "glory," rays of light that emanate outward. The symbol of the Eye was first incorporated as part of the Great Seal in 1782 and is grouped with the words "Annuit Coeptis," which can be interpreted as saying America is favored or supported by God.

▼ The image of the Great Seal of the United States appears on the dollar bill, some say at the instigation of Freemason President Franklin D. Roosevelt.

At the base of the pyramid appear the words "Novus Ordo Seclorum," declaring that America is a "New Secular Order," formed like a pyramid of a broad base of people surmounted and watched over by the Eye of Providence. The obverse side of the Great Seal also features symbolism that can be found in Freemasonry. A glory that once again symbolizes God surrounds the 13 stars of the United States. Beneath the glory is a picture of an eagle that is said to represent the spirit and carries the arrows of war alongside the laurel wreath signifying peace. The Great Seal can be found on the American dollar bill. Some have claimed that it was President Franklin D. Roosevelt, himself a Freemason, who put forward the idea in 1935 that the Great Seal appear on the bill.

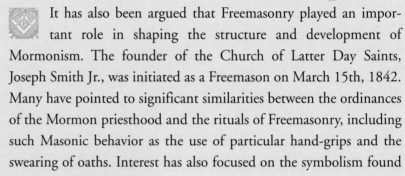

# Freemasonry and Mormonism

▲ Freemasons can recognize each other by their distinctive handshake.

▶ Salt Lake City Temple, the most important Mormon church, abounds with Masonic symbolism.

▼ Joseph Smith, founder of the Church of the Latter Day Saints and the Mormon religion.

It has also been argued that Freemasonry played an important role in shaping the structure and development of Mormonism. The founder of the Church of Latter Day Saints, Joseph Smith Jr., was initiated as a Freemason on March 15th, 1842. Many have pointed to significant similarities between the ordinances of the Mormon priesthood and the rituals of Freemasonry, including such Masonic behavior as the use of particular hand-grips and the swearing of oaths. Interest has also focused on the symbolism found in the Salt Lake City Temple, which many argue derives from the world of Freemasonry. The all-seeing eye and the use of the five-pointed star are examples of images and ideas that can be found in Masonic symbolism.

In fact, the architecture of the temples of The Church of Latter Day Saints, like Masonic lodges, contains many references and influences from the biblical descriptions of the legendary Temple of Solomon. Every Mormon temple currently in use incorporates a baptismal font that is designed after the manner of the Brazen Sea that is described in I Kings. The fonts within Mormon temples are upheld by 12 figurines of oxen. Many important leaders within the Church of Latter Day Saints were

also Freemasons, including Brigham Young, the second president of Mormonism, and his father and brothers.

It has been argued that Smith's connection to Freemasonry is borne out by the circumstances surrounding his death. He was killed in 1844 and it is said that, just before he was shot, he raised both hands in the air and cried out "The Lord and my God." Some have speculated that this was not simply a final appeal to God for help but was, in fact, a phrase taken from Masonry, one used when a Mason is appealing to any other Masons who might be present for their help in a time of danger.

▲ Brigham Young, the second Mormon leader, was also a Freemason.

▶ The Mormon Temple in Oakland California, dedicated in 1964, is an East Bay landmark and is redolent of Freemasonry in its design and symbolism.

# Freemasonry Today

In recent years attempts have been made in Britain to force members of fraternal societies in positions of public office to declare their membership of such groups, prompted by high profile cases of Masons involved in illegal activities However, this was challenged under European human rights legislation and the government was forced to limit its policy. In 1999 the Police Service introduced a system whereby Freemasons in the force can voluntarily make their membership public. There is currently no definitive listing available of individuals who are members of Freemasonic organizations.

▲ Camilla, Duchess of Cornwall, thanks leading members of the United Grand Lodge of England for their charitable donation to a London hospital.

The fears and concerns that secret societies continue to provoke are best demonstrated by the ways in which such groups are depicted in popular culture. Fascination with esoteric groups that hold secret knowledge, hidden from the general public, which provides them with an alternative view of history, informs the works of many popular novelists, although not all such representations are negative. It is worrying that such theories, usually based on paranoia and intrigue, can become focused on groups such as the Freemasons. It can be argued that conspiracy theories believed by such figures as Henry Ford led ultimately to the mass persecution of Masons under the Nazi regime. Today, the popularity of Freemasonry is in decline, as fewer and fewer young people become members. This is in stark contrast with a growing public obsession with the myths and legends attached to Freemasonry. It seems likely that Freemasons will continue to be viewed as the "men who control the world." The reality is that Freemasons the world over continue to work quietly for the benefit not only of their members but for the wider good.

# Reference

# MYSTERIVM MAGNVM
## STVDIVM VNIVERSALI.

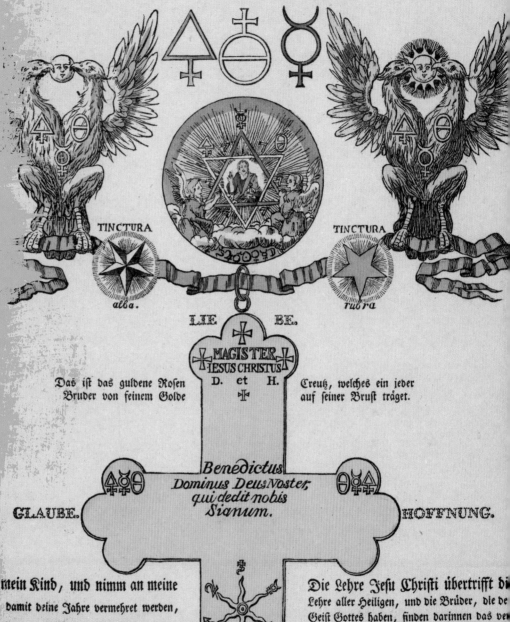

TINCTURA

TINCTURA

*alba.*

*rubra.*

LIE. BE.

MAGISTER
IESUS CHRISTUS
D. et H.

Das ist das guldene Rosen
Bruder von seinem Golde

Creutz, welches ein jeder
auf seiner Brust träget.

*Benedictus
Dominus Deus Noster,
qui dedit nobis
Signum.*

GLAUBE.

HOFFNUNG.

mein Kind, und nimm an meine

damit deine Jahre vermehret werden,

will dir den Weg der Weißheit zeigen,

führen durch die Bahn der Gerechtig-

an du darauf gehen wirst, so sollen

e Gänge nicht beängstiget werden, und

geschwinde lauffest, wirst du nicht an-

Halte die Lehre, und bewahre

ie ist dein Leben. Prov. IV. v. 10.

Die Lehre Jesu Christi übertrifft di

Lehre aller Heiligen, und die Brüder, die de

Geist Gottes haben, finden darinnen das ve

borgene Himmel-Brod, und den Stein de

Weisen, ☿. ♃. ☉. Es geschiehet aber, da

viele Menschen, ob sie schon oft das Evange

lium und die Sprache der Weisen hören, jedoc

keine Begierde daraus empfinden, denn sie ha

ben den Geist Christi nicht. Wer aber di

Worte Christi verstehen will, und der Weise

Reden ergründen, der muß sich befleißigen, m

seinem Leben Christo gleichförmig zu werden.

*Frater
Rosæ et Aureæ
Crucis*

GED ULT.

TINCTUR.

Ich will dir grosse und gewaltige Dinge zeigen.

# Appendix: The Scottish and York Rites

## The 32 Degrees of the Scottish Rite

### The Ineffable Degrees

The first ten degrees within the Scottish Rite are known as the Ineffable Degrees and are:

### Fourth Degree—Secret Master

The candidate learns that in order to fulfill his duties it is at times necessary to be able to keep secrets and remain trustworthy.

### Fifth Degree—Perfect Master

This degree teaches the importance of revering and respecting our forebears and stresses the need to behave honorably. The murder of Hiram Abiff is an important part of the symbolism in the degree of Perfect Master.

### Sixth Degree—Intimate Secretary

Masons are instructed that they should not involve themselves unduly in the affairs of their fellow Masons. The degree is based on a story about King Solomon intervening to protect a Mason who had been accused of spying.

### Seventh Degree—Provost and Judge

This degree teaches the importance of fairness and equality within any system of justice and that Masons should behave honorably and mercifully. Its symbolic context is the trial of the murderers of Hiram Abiff.

## Eighth Degree—Intendant of the Building

The theme of the Intendant of the Building is charity and helping the less fortunate in society. Its allegorical backdrop is the resumption of the construction of the Temple of Solomon after the murder of Hiram Abiff.

## Ninth Degree—Elect of the Nine

The title of the degree refers to King Solomon choosing nine Masons to find the murderers of Hiram Abiff. It teaches the importance of serving others within society.

## Tenth Degree—Elect of the Fifteen

Candidates are shown that justice will triumph in the end over unfair and unrighteous actions. Its symbolic context is the trial of the murderers of Hiram Abiff.

## Eleventh Degree—Elect of the Twelve

Masons who show honesty and fairness and behave with honor will reap the rewards of their actions, just as unbecoming or corrupt actions will result in punishment through fair and impartial justice.

## Twelfth Degree—Grand Master Architect

This degree uses the allegorical symbolism of the education of the builders of the Temple of King Solomon to instruct Masons in their role within the world and to teach them how to respect the work of the Great Architect.

## Thirteenth Degree—Royal Arch of Solomon

This concerns the difficulties and hardships that may face a Mason in striving for perfection. It teaches that the achievement of high goals is through persistent and, at times, difficult struggle and labor.

### Fourteenth Degree—Grand Elect Perfect and Sublime

Once a Mason has reached this stage within the Scottish Rite, he has been fully prepared to construct his own metaphorical lodge of perfection. In this degree the candidate discovers that a hidden chamber was built under the Temple of Solomon to house a precious artifact referred to as the pillar of beauty.

## The Chapter of the Rose Croix

The next sequence of degrees is the Chapter of the Rose Croix. The symbolic context in which moral lessons are taught to Masons is the captivity of the Jews in Babylon and their eventual return to Jerusalem.

### Fifteenth Degree—Knight of the East or Sword

Candidates learn that it is essential to retain their integrity and beliefs and not to be dissuaded from them.

### Sixteenth Degree—Prince of Jerusalem

When the Jews returned to Jerusalem they undertook the building of the Second Temple and faced hardship, often having to fight for their

▶ The statue of George Washington in the Memorial Hall of the Masonic National Memorial in Alexandria, Virginia, which was dedicated in 1932 in recognition of the first president of the United States, a Freemason, George Washington.

freedom. Masons learn that they must meet their responsibilities even in the face of hardship and danger.

**Seventeenth Degree—Knight of the East and West**
This degree acknowledges that the lasting Temple to the Great Architect lies not in the material world but within the spiritual world.

**Eighteenth Degree—Knight Rose Croix**
The ultimate degree of the Chapter of the Rose Croix instructs Masons to build a temple to God within themselves and concerns the Rosicrucian themes of transforming society through the transformation of our own souls.

## The Council of Kadosh
The next stage within the Scottish Rite is referred to as the Council of Kadosh and runs from the Nineteenth to the Thirtieth Degrees:

**Nineteenth Degree—Grand Pontiff**
The theme of this is that the Mason should look beyond individual creeds and religions and that those who believe in a divine power and the immortality of the soul are as one.

**Twentieth Degree—Master ad Vitam**
This degree deals with the problems and requirements of leadership. It stresses the importance of individuals working together to improve society.

**Twenty-first Degree—Patriarch Noachite**
This emphasizes that Masons must not abuse their position within Freemasonry and must behave honorably and within the law. It also teaches respect for justice correctly and fairly administered.

**Twenty-second Degree—Prince of Libanus**

This degree takes its title from an ancient name for the country of Lebanon. In the story of the building of the Temple of Solomon the cedar wood used in its construction came from Lebanon. The degree teaches the value and the honor inherent in hard work through the allegorical framework of cutting wood.

**Twenty-third Degree—Chief of the Tabernacle**

The Mason is reminded to strive always to give aid to his fellows and to perform good works in recognition of the Great Architect.

**Twenty-fourth Degree—Prince of the Tabernacle**

This illustrates how peoples around the world, apparently from differing cultures, actually have much in common. Through the study of symbolism Masons must learn to recognize these universal concerns and promote cooperation and mutual aid and respect.

**Twenty-fifth Degree—Knight of the Brazen Serpent**

This degree recognizes that all people must suffer hardships but that good will triumph over evil.

**Twenty-sixth Degree—Prince of Mercy**

The subject of this degree is showing mercy and understanding to others even if they have offended or wronged us. Justice and any accompanying punishment should always be administered with this in mind.

**Twenty-seventh Degree—Commander of the Temple**

This degree is based on what is known of the crusading order known as the Teutonic Knights of the House of St. Mary of Jerusalem. The order performed the dual function of providing medical assistance and serving as warriors.

## Twenty-eighth Degree—Knight of the Sun

The degree of the Knight of the Sun is strongly influenced by the Kabbalah and the concept of the Tree of Life.

## Twenty-ninth Degree—Knight of St. Andrew

The Mason is shown the importance of treating the ideas and beliefs of others with respect and the degree encourages a spirit of tolerance within humanity.

## Thirtieth Degree—Knight Kadosh

The final degree in the Council of Kadosh, this teaches that the difficulties that we face improve us as people and that Masons must strive to protect the metaphorical internal temple within themselves that they have built through their Masonic training.

## The Consistory

This is the final stage within the Scottish Rite and runs from the thirty-first to the thirty-third degrees.

## Thirty-first Degree—Inspector Inquisitor Commander

This degree concerns justice and the recognition that all people must judge their own weaknesses and failings before judging others. Once again, the administration of fair and appropriate justice must be accompanied with compassion and understanding.

## Thirty-second Degree—Sublime Prince of the Royal Secret

This degree examines the difference between our physical selves and our spiritual beings. It teaches that the spiritual can overcome selfishness and self-interest through struggle and that Masons may have to make great sacrifices to help others.

**Thirty-third Degree—Knight Commander of the Court of Honor**
This is an honorary degree and may not be applied for. It can be awarded only by fellow Masons, usually for an outstanding achievement or contribution.

## The Three Stages of the York Rite

The York Rite also offers an opportunity for Master Masons to progress further within the world of Freemasonry beyond the standard three degrees of Blue Lodge Masonry. It is found mainly as a single system in America and there are differences within the different orders that teach it. There are three stages within the York Rite that a Master Mason is first eligible to join:

### Royal Arch Masonry

This order is also referred to as the Chapter, indicating a group of Royal Arch Masons. Within this order candidates may undertake the Mark Master Mason degree. It takes its name and symbolism from the practice of medieval masons carving individual symbols upon the structures and stonework for which they were responsible so that they might be recognized by other masons.

The next degree within Royal Arch Masonry is that of Virtual Past Master. This is followed by the degree of Most Excellent Master and is unique within Freemasonry in that its imagery is the completion of King Solomon's Temple.

The final degree in the sequence is that of the Royal Arch Mason. This is very often termed the "most beautiful," "sublime," or "elegant" degree within Freemasonry.

### Cryptic Masonry

Those who reach this elevated Masonic degree are eligible, but not obliged, to undertake the degrees of Cryptic Masonry. The degrees within the Cryptic Rite are those of Royal Master, Select Master, and Super Excellent Master. It derives this secondary term of identification because some type of underground chamber or crypt-like room forms a part of the developing degrees that it encompasses.

## The Commandery of Knights Templar

The third and final body within the York Rite is unusual in Masonic groups in that its membership does require a specific religious belief system. While Freemasonry in general is open to individuals with a belief in a supreme being, the degree of Knights Templar is open only to Master Masons whose religion is Christianity.

▼ The ultimate degree of the Commandery of Knights Templar resonates with the symbolism of the medieval Order of Templars.

# Glossary

**Allegiance**—A Mason owes allegiance first to the Lodge of which he is a member; second, to the Grand Lodge under which the Lodge is chartered; and, ultimately, to the supreme body or Grand Lodge.

**All-Seeing Eye**—An ever-present symbol in the Lodge and work of Freemasonry, this signifies the omnipresence and omniscience of God.

**Altar**—The altar occupies the central place in the lodge room of Freemasons. Lying upon the altar is the Holy Bible, which remains open during the work of the lodge. It is at the altar that Masons kneel and assume the oaths and obligations of the several degrees.

**Apron**—The use of an apron as a mystic symbol has been common among Ancient Masons. In the first degree, the initiate is presented with the pure white lambskin apron as a reminder that purity of life and conduct are essentially necessary to gaining admission to the Celestial Lodge above where the Supreme Architect of the Universe resides forever. This apron becomes his permanent property as the "badge of a Freemason." As he advances in Masonry, he may receive other aprons of varying types, but never one that holds such significance and Masonic value.

**Ark of the Covenant**—This is said to have been kept in The Most Holy Place in the Tabernacle erected by Moses on Mount Sinai. Legend says that it contained the Book of Law, the stone tablets on which God had written the Ten Commandments, a pot of manna, and Aaron's rod (the staff carried by Aaron, brother of and assistant to Moses, as a token of his office—it miraculously blossomed as evidence of his divine choice as High Priest).

**Brought to Light**—A term used in Masonic degree rituals to describe the moment when a candidate has his hoodwink (blindfold) removed, with implications of a more profound enlightenment.

**Cardinal Virtues**—These are the preeminent virtues on which all others hinge. As set forth in the Entered Apprentice degree, they are Temperance, Fortitude, Prudence, and Justice.

**Column**—Three columns are employed to signify the supports of a Lodge: the columns of Wisdom, Strength, and Beauty.

**Cornerstone**—This is the stone that lies at the corner of two walls of a building in which, by tradition, certain historic documents are placed and on which inscriptions are engraved. In Masonic buildings, it is always placed at the northeast corner.

**Covenant of Masons**—In becoming a Mason, a man enters into a covenant with the Fraternity, agreeing to fulfill certain promises and perform certain duties. At the same time, the Fraternity and its members bind themselves to certain ties of friendship, brotherliness, protection, support, and benefits. The breaking of a covenant is taken seriously and is subject to stated penalties.

**Craft**—Another term for Masonry, implying that there are certain skills to be learned and developed within a system of apprenticeship and mastery.

**Craftsmen**—The term "craft" applies to persons collectively engaged in a trade or mechanical operation. It is used of operative Masons, and the majority of those employed in the building of the Temple were thus referred to as craftsmen. In speculative Masonry, the entire Brotherhood is spoken of as the Craft, and individual members as Craftsmen.

**Creation**—All Freemasons recognise Jehovah as God and as the Great Architect of the Universe, the creator of all things, material and spiritual. They accept the account of Creation given in the Book of Genesis and confirmed by other Scriptures.

**Deacons**—In every Masonic lodge there are two officers known as the Senior and Junior Deacons. Their duties cover general surveillance over the lodge, the introduction of visitors, and serving as proxy for the Worshipful Master in certain circumstances.

**Entered Apprentice**—An initiate of the first degree in Masonry. Entered Apprentices are charged to work primarily at improving their moral character. Their tools include the 24-inch gauge and the common gavel.

**Fellowcraft**—A Fellowcraft, or Craftsman, is a Mason who has been passed to the second degree of Masonry. Craftsmen are charged to continue their moral improvement, while also improving their minds through study of the classic seven liberal arts and sciences, especially geometry. The tools of Craftsmen include the plumb, square, and level.

**Gates of the Temple**—The Temple of Solomon had only one entrance, but the walls of the enclosure had a gate at each point of the compass. Freemasonry makes special symbolic use of three of these gates, which represent the symbols of the progress of the sun, rising in the east, reaching its zenith in the south, and setting in the west. They are said to symbolize birth, life, and death, as well as youth, manhood, and old age.

**Gnosticism**—This is the doctrine that knowledge (Greek *gnosis*) is the way to salvation. It was developed in the Gnostic schools of the second century A.D., some of which had associations with the early Christian community.

**Grand Architect of the Universe**—also called the Great or Supreme Architect. This is a term used by Masons to refer to the Supreme Being, also referred to in Masonic ritual as the Creator, Deity, and God. Masons are required to profess a belief in a Supreme Being, but according to Anderson's Constitutions of 1723 every Mason has the right to maintain his own beliefs and religion thus ensuring that every great religion of humanity is represented within the fraternity of Masonry.

**Hermetic Tradition**—A body of Hellenistic mystical philosophy of the second and third centuries A.D., which was named after Hermes Trismegistus (the Egyptian god Thoth), whose teachings are revealed as the way of wisdom and life.

**Hiram Abiff**—Grand Master Hiram Abiff was said to be the son of a widow sent to King Solomon to serve as the Chief Architect of Solomon's Temple. In Masonic tradition it is said that three fellow Craftsmen desired to know the secrets of a Master Mason, and that they murdered Hiram when he refused to reveal them. In Masonry his associations are with the office of Junior Warden, the Pillar of Beauty, and the South of the Lodge.

**Holy of Holies**—The Tabernacle erected by Moses at Mount Sinai, which was divided into two compartments or rooms; at the west end was the Most Holy Place—also known as the Sanctum Sanctorum—constructed as a perfect cube, 15 feet in all dimensions. It was separated from the other room, the Holy Place, by curtains. The only article of furniture in the Holy of Holies was the Ark of the Covenant. Similarly, King Solomon's Temple was divided into two compartments, and there, the Most Holy Place was a perfect cube, 40 feet in all its dimensions, and the walls and floor were overlaid with fine gold. As in the tabernacle, the only article of furniture was the Ark of the Covenant.

**King Hiram of Tyre**—According to Masonic tradition, many of the workers and materials required for the building of King Solomon's Temple were supplied by King Hiram. In Freemasonry this Grand Master is associated with the the office of Senior Warden, the Pillar of Strength, and the West of the Lodge.

**King Solomon**—According to the Bible Solomon was the son of King David, and the builder of the first Temple in Jerusalem. Solomon was renowned for his wisdom and for serving the people of Israel, and was credited with the authorship of the Song of Songs. In Masonry this Grand Master is associated with the office of Worshipful Master, the Pillar of Wisdom, and the East of the Lodge.

**Master Mason**—The term denotes one who has been raised to the third degree of Masonry, which is also known as the "Sublime Degree." In addition to continuing the work they began as Entered Apprentices and Fellow Craftsmen, they are also required to act as agents of brotherly love and to seek the Lost Word. The tools of Master Masons include all the instruments of Masonry, but especially the trowel.

**Master of the Lodge**—The Master of the Lodge is required to be fully informed in the principles of Freemasonry. Masonry is a science of morals, steeped in symbolism, mystery, and allegory, and any Mason who becomes a teacher (denoted by the title Master of the Lodge) of this science must fully understand all of these aspects of the craft.

**The Two Pillars**—King Solomon's Temple had two giant bronze shafts, which stood in front of the entrance to the Great Porch at the eastern entrance of the Temple. Each of these pillars was 70 feet in height and 24 feet in circumference and they were elaborately decorated with brass wreaths and bronze pomegranates. These two great pillars were given the names Boaz and Jachin.

**Pillars of Wisdom**—The seven great pillars of wisdom – rhetoric, grammar, geometry, music, mathematics, astronomy, and logic, are regarded by Masons as being of superlative worth in the building of a moral and spiritual world.

**Priory of Sion**—Historically an obscure traditional Catholic chivalric order founded during the Fourth Republic in France, but now more commonly associated with a mystical secret society whose aim was to restore the Merovingian dynasty to the thrones of Europe and Jerusalem, an idea popularized in books such as *The Holy Blood and the Holy Grail*.

**Resurrection**—Freemasonry is built on two cardinal beliefs: a belief in God, and belief in a resurrection to a future life, and these fundamental beliefs are expressed through its rituals and symbols and in all of its teachings, myths, and legends.

**Sabbath Day**—In common with all of the major religions, Freemasonry recognizes the requirement for one day's rest from the ordinary weekly toils of life. This is recognized in the Sabbath Day, which is reserved as a day of rest and Divine Worship.

**St. John the Baptist**—all Freemasons acknowledge and honor St. John the Baptist as the forerunner of the Messiah and Savior and his name is associated with a number of significant rituals.

**St. John the Evangelist**—A disciple of St. John the Baptist, John the Evangelist was a son of Zebedee and brother of James, and was numbered among the earliest to follow Jesus. He was one of the 12 Apostles and the author of five New Testament books: the Gospel bearing his name; three Epistles; and the Book of Revelation of. He is highly honored in Masonic tradition and rituals.

**Ten Commandments**—Freemasons acknowledge the Ten Commandments as being of divine origin and accept them as the moral code by which all human relations with God and with mankind should be governed.

**Tyler**—The symbolism of the workman of operative Masonry known as the Tyler (spelt Tiler in some jurisdictions), is invested in the office of Tyler (spelt Tiler in some jurisdictions) in speculative Masonry. The Tyler's duty is to provide protection for the Lodge when it is organized and ready for business, closing the doors and keeping away intruders.

**Wages**—Masons who worked on the construction of King Solomon's Temple would have been paid wages, although there is no specific reference to this in the Bible. In speculative Masonry certain labors are performed, the reward or wages for which are spiritual.

**Winding Stairs**—Within the Temple of Solomon there was an impressive winding stairway, which consisted of 15 steps leading from the porch to the second floor. The winding staircase in Freemasonry alludes to this and is one of its enduring symbols.

**Wisdom of Solomon**—In Ancient Craft Masonry, King Solomon was the exemplar of the highest degree of wisdom. Today the Wisdom of Solomon symbolizes for every Freemason the wisdom needed to attain success in life.

**Worshipful Master**—As the chief officer of a lodge the Master of the Lodge is called worshipful because, of all lodge members, he is the one who should be most reverent, humble, and aware of his need for guidance from the Grand Architect of the Universe.

# Bibliography

*The Holy Bible: New Revised Standard Version*, Oxford: Oxford University Press, 1995

Baigent, Michael, Leigh, Richard & Lincoln, Henry, *The Holy Blood & The Holy Grail*, London: Arrow Books, 1982

Baigent, Michael & Leigh, Richard, *The Temple and the Lodge*, London: Arrow Books, 1998

Brighton, Simon, *In Search of the Knights Templar*, London: Weidenfeld & Nicolson, 2006

Brown, Dan, *The Da Vinci Code*, London: Bantam Press, 2004

Carr, Harry, *The Freemasons at Work*, Shepperton: Lewis Masonic, 1992

Cooper, D. Jason, *Mithras: Mysteries and Initiation Rediscovered*, Newburyport, Mass.: Samuel Weiser Inc., 1996

Duncan, Malcolm C., *Duncan's Ritual of Freemasonry*, New York: Crown, 1976

Dedopulos, Tim, *The Brotherhood*, London: Carlton Books, 2006

Hamill, John, *The Craft: A History of English Freemasonry*, London: Crucible, 1986

Harwood, Jeremy, *The Freemasons*, London: Hermes House, 2006

Jeffers, H. Paul, Freemasons: *Inside the World's Oldest Secret Society*, New York: Citadel Press, 2005

Johnstone, Michael, *The Freemasons: The Illustrated Book of an Ancient Brotherhood*, London: Arcturus, 2005

Knight, Christopher & Lomas, Robert, *The Hiram Key*, London: Arrow Books, 1997

Knight, Christopher & Lomas, Robert, *Turning the Hiram Key*, London: Lewis Masonic, 2005

Lomas, Robert, *The Secrets of Freemasonry: Revealing the Suppressed Tradition*, London: Robinson, 2006

MacNulty, W. Kirk, *Freemasonry: Symbols, Secrets, Significance*, London: Thames & Hudson, 2006

MacNulty, W. Kirk, Freemasonry: *A Journey Through Ritual and Symbol*, London: Thames & Hudson, 1994

Martin, Sean, *The Knights Templar*, London: Pocket Essentials, 2004

Mavromataki, Maria, *Greek Mythology and Religion*, Athens: Haitalis, 1997

Nicholson, Helen, *The Knights Hospitaller*, Woodbridge, Suffolk: Boydell, 2001

Porter, Lindsay, *Who Are The Illuminati?* London: Collins & Brown, 2005

Read, Piers Paul, *The Templars*, London: Phoenix Press, 2001

## Text credits

# Index